Concepts for Today

A High Intermediate
Reading Skills Text

Concepts for Today

A High Intermediate Reading Skills Text

Lorraine C. Smith
Nancy Nici Mare

English Language Institute
Queens College
The City University of New York

Illustrations by
Joseph Tenga

Heinle & Heinle Publishers
A Division of Wadsworth Inc.
Boston, Massachusetts 02116 U.S.A.

The publication of *Concepts for Today: A High Intermediate Reading Skills Text* was directed by the members of the Newbury House Publishing Team at Heinle & Heinle:

Erik Gundersen, Editorial Director
Susan Mraz, Marketing Director
Gabrielle B. McDonald, Production Editor

Also participating in the publication of this program were:
Publisher: Stanley J. Galek
Editorial Production Manager: Elizabeth Holthaus
Project Manager: LeGwin Associates
Associate Editor: Lynne Telson Barsky
Associate Marketing Manager: Donna Hamilton
Production Assistant: Maryellen Eschmann
Manufacturing Coordinator: Mary Beth Lynch
Photo Coordinator: Martha Leibs-Heckly
Cover Designer: Christy Russo

ESL
READING
SMi
1994

Photo Credits
p. 2, © Ulrike Welsch
p. 5, © Michael Lajoie
p. 56, © Superstock, Inc.
p. 111, © Perry Werner/The Image Works
p. 112, © Margot Granitsas/The Image Works
p. 117, © Edith Reichmann/Monkmeyer Press Photo Service
p. 121, © Superstock, Inc.
p. 173, © Superstock, Inc.
pp. 178, 179, © Ira Kirschenbaum/Stock, Boston
p. 190, ©Hanny Paul/The Gamma Liaison Network
p. 208, © Topham Picture Library/The Image Works

Photographs and mechanical art by Joseph Tenga on pp. 1, 13, 15, 18, 21, 28, 31, 32, 33, 39, 55, 56, 59, 66, 70, 75, 94, 103, 107, 111, 133, 136, 146, 150, 166, 174, 200, 206, 207, 213, 219

Heinle & Heinle Publishers is a division of Wadsworth, Inc.

Manufactured in the United States of America

ISBN: 0-8384-3436-3

10 9 8 7 6

To our parents: Peg and Smitty; Anthony and Antoinette

Contents

Preface

Concepts for Today is a reading skills text intended for high-intermediate, college-bound students of English as a second or foreign language. The passages in this book have been selected from original articles published in a wide variety of periodicals and newspapers allowing students the opportunity to read authentic materials from American publications. As they engage with the materials in each chapter of this book, students develop the kinds of extensive and intensive reading skills they will need to achieve academic success in English.

Concepts for Today is one in a series of four reading skills texts. The complete series has been designed to meet the needs of students from the high beginning to the advanced levels and includes the following:

- *Insights for Today* .... high beginning
- *Issues for Today* .... intermediate
- *Concepts for Today* .... high intermediate
- *Topics for Today* .... advanced

Concepts for Today provides students with essential practice in the type of reading skills they will need in an academic environment. It requires students not only to read text, but also to examine information from various forms of charts, graphs, illustrations, and photographs. Furthermore, students are given the opportunity to speak and write about their own experiences, country, and culture in English and to compare these experiences and ideas with those of people from the United States and other countries.

This thematically-organized text consists of four units, each containing three chapters that deal with related subjects. This organization provides for a natural recycling of content-specific vocabulary and concepts and discipline-specific sentence structure and rhetorical patterns. It should be noted that though all three chapters in each unit are linked by theme, they can as easily be taught individually as in concert with one another. For the instructor who chooses to teach all three chapters in each unit, there is a unit-ending vocabulary review and discussion section that ties together the three related topics.

The initial exercise preceding each reading encourages the students to think about the ideas, facts, and vocabulary that will be presented in the passage. Discussing illustrations in class helps students visualize what they are going to read about and gives them cues for the new vocabulary they will encounter. The exercises that follow the reading passage are intended to develop and improve reading proficiency, including the ability to learn new vocabulary from context and to develop comprehension of English sentence structure, and study skills such as note-taking, proper dictionary use, and library research. The follow-up activities give students the opportunity to master useful vocabulary encountered in the articles through discussion and group work, and lead the students to a comprehension of main ideas and specific information.

As students work through the text, they will learn and improve reading skills, and also develop confidence in their growing English proficiency. At the same time, the teacher will be able to observe their steady progress toward skillful, independent reading.

Acknowledgements

We gratefully acknowledge the generous support of our editor, Erik Gundersen, and the help and enthusiasm of the teachers, staff, and students of the ELI at Queens College in the preparation, testing, and revision of this manuscript.

L.C.S. and N.N.M.

Introduction

How to Use This Book

Each chapter in this book consists of the following:

Prereading Preparation
Reading Passage
Fact-Finding Scanning Exercise
Reading Analysis
Word Form Exercise
Dictionary Skills
Information Organization
Information Organization Quiz and Summary
Critical Thinking Strategies
Follow-up Discussion and Activities

In order to get the students out of the classroom and give them the chance to use English in the real world, there are surveys in the follow-up activities section of several chapters. A Library Resource Mastery section is included in Chapters 3, 4, 6, 7, 9, 10, and 11. The library work affords the students practice in developing valuable library research skills they will need in a full-time academic environment. Each unit contains a vocabulary categorization exercise, a crossword puzzle, and unit discussion questions. Both the vocabulary exercise and the crossword puzzle incorporate vocabulary from all three chapters in the unit. The discussion section at the end of each unit ties in the related topics of the three chapters. There is a quiz in each chapter that is based on the information organization practice. In addition, there is a Cloze quiz for each chapter, located at the end of the book. This gives the teacher the option of removing the entire test section from all the students' books at the beginning of the term and giving out each test as the class finishes each chapter. The Answer Key for all exercises, including the Cloze tests, is at the end of the Pullout Section and may also be removed by the teacher at the beginning of the term.

The format of each chapter in the book is consistent. Although each chapter can be done entirely in class, some exercises may be assigned for homework. This, of course, depends on the individual teacher's preference, as well as the availability of class time.

Prereading Preparation

This prereading activity is designed to stimulate student interest and provide preliminary vocabulary for the passage itself. The importance of prereading preparation should not be underestimated. Studies have shown the positive effect of prereading preparation in motivating student interest, activating background knowledge, and enhancing reading comprehension. Time should be spent describing and discussing the illustrations as well as discussing the title and the prereading questions. Furthermore, the students should try to relate the topic to their own experience and try to predict what they are going to read about.

The Reading Passage

As the students read the passage for the first time, they should be encouraged to read *ideas*. In English, ideas are in groups of words, in sentences, and in paragraphs, not in individual words.

Fact-Finding Scanning Exercise

After the first reading, the students will read the True/False statements, then go back to the passage and scan for the information that will clarify whether each statement is true or false. If the statement is false, the students will rewrite the statement so that it becomes true. This activity can be done individually or in groups.

Reading Analysis

The students will read each question and answer it. This exercise deals with vocabulary from context, transition words, punctuation clues, sentence structure, sentence comprehension, and pronoun referents. The teacher should review personal and relative pronouns before doing this section. This exercise may be assigned for homework, or it may be done in class individually or in groups, giving the students the opportunity to discuss their reasons for their answers.

Word Forms

As an introduction to the word form exercises in this book, it is recommended that the teacher first review parts of speech, especially verbs, nouns, adjectives, and adverbs. Teachers should point out each word form's position in a sentence. Students will develop a sense for which part of speech is missing in a given sentence. Teachers should also point out clues to tense and number, and to whether an idea is affirmative or negative. The teacher can do the example with the students before the exercise or as an assignment after the exercise is completed. Each section has its own instructions, depending on the particular pattern that is being introduced. For example, in the section containing words that take *-tion* in the noun form, the teacher can explain that in this exercise the students will look at the verb and noun forms of two types of words that use the suffix *-tion* in their noun form. (1) Some words simply add *-tion* to the verb: *suggest/suggestion*; if the word ends in *-e*, the *-e* is dropped first: *produce/production*; (2) other words drop the final *e* and add *-ation*: *examine/examination*. This exercise is very effective when done in pairs. After students have a working knowledge of this type of exercise, it can be assigned for homework.

Dictionary Skills

This exercise provides students with much needed practice in selecting the appropriate dictionary entry for an unknown word, depending on the context. In each of the first six chapters, the students are given entries from the *Oxford ESL Dictionary for Students of American English* for several words from the reading in that chapter. The sentence containing the dictionary word is provided below the entry. The student selects the appropriate entry and writes the entry number and the definition or synonym into the sentence in the space provided. The students should write the answer in a grammatically correct form, since they may not always copy verbatim from the dictionary. In Chapters 7–12, the format is the same, but the entries are from *Webster's Ninth New Collegiate Dictionary*. The students can work in pairs on this exercise and report back to the class. They should be prepared to justify their choices.

Information Organization

In this exercise, students are asked to read the passage a second time, take notes, and organize the information they have just read. They may be asked to complete an outline, a table, or a flowchart. The teacher may want to review the concept of note-taking before beginning the exercise. The outline, table, or flowchart can be sketched on the blackboard by the teacher or a student and completed by individual students in front of the class. Variations can be discussed by the class as a group. It should be pointed out to the students that in American colleges, teachers often base their exams on the notes that students are expected to take during class lectures and that they, too, will be tested on *their* notes.

Information Organization Quiz and Summary

This quiz is based on the notes the students took in the Information Organization exercise. Students should be instructed to read the questions and then refer to their notes to answer them. They are also asked to write a summary of the article. The teacher may want to review how to summarize. This section can be a written assignment to be done as homework or as an actual test. Alternately, it can be prepared in class and discussed.

Critical Thinking Strategies

The students refer back to parts of the article and think about the implications of the information or comments it contains. There are also questions about the author's purpose and tone. The goal of the exercise is for students to form their own ideas and opinions on aspects of the topic discussed. The students can work on these questions as individual writing exercises or in a small group discussion activity.

Follow-up Discussion and Activities

This section contains various activities appropriate to the information in the passages. Some activities are designed for pair and small-group work. Students are encouraged to use the information and vocabulary from the passages both orally and in writing. The teacher may also use these questions and activities as homework or in-class assignments.

Library Resource Mastery

In order to do the assignments in this section, each student will need a valid public library card or a student I.D. card in order to use the campus library.

The library resource mastery sections in this text help students develop library research skills. Each segment addresses a specific aspect of searching for information, for example, using the card catalog to locate a book, using the *Reader's Guide to Periodical Literature* to find material in periodicals, or using reference books to find specific information. Each assignment asks the students to do further research on topics related to each unit, just as they will do when enrolled in college courses.

The most important point for the students to keep in mind when using any library is that the librarians are there to help them. As foreign students, they may not be familiar with the American library system. Consequently, they may need some assistance until they become accustomed to using the library. It is part of a librarian's job to help people, and librarians are usually very willing to lend students any assistance they may need. They should feel free to ask for help if they need it.

Index of Key Words and Phrases

This section contains words and phrases from all the chapters for easy reference. It is located after the last chapter.

Pullout Section

Cloze Quiz

The Cloze quiz is a section of the passage itself, but with words missing. The Cloze quiz tests not only vocabulary, but also sentence structure and general comprehension. The students are given the missing words that are to be filled in the blank spaces. The quiz for each chapter is placed at the end of the book in the Pullout Section. The teacher has the option of collecting the entire pullout section of quizzes, including the Answer Key, from the students at the beginning of the semester. In this way, the teacher will have a copy of all the quizzes for each student in the class and can administer the quizzes after each chapter is covered. The quizzes can be done either as a test or as a group assignment.

Answer Key

The Answer Key is located at the end of the book and provides the answers for the exercises, the end-of-unit vocabulary review, and the Cloze quizzes.

Living in Society

C·H·A·P·T·E·R 1

The Paradox of Happiness

by Diane Swanbrow
Psychology Today

• Prereading Preparation

1. a. In groups of three, write a definition of **happy.** Write what it means to be happy. On the blackboard, compare your definitions with the definitions of the other groups in the class.
   b. Do the same for **unhappy.**
   c. Compare your class explanations of **happy** and **unhappy**. Are they opposites? Is there a relationship between happiness and unhappiness?
2. What makes you happy? When do you feel happy?
3. What makes you feel unhappy?
4. a. Are you a happy person?
   b. Do you come from a happy family?
5. Do you think your environment can cause you to be happy or unhappy? Explain your answer.
6. Look at the title of this article. What is a **paradox**? Why might there be a paradox involving happiness and unhappiness?

1   It's plain common sense—the more happiness you feel,
2 the less unhappiness you experience. It's plain common
3 sense, but it's not true. Recent research reveals that happi-
4 ness and unhappiness are not really flip sides of the same
5 emotion. They are two distinct feelings that, coexisting,
6 rise and fall independently.
7   "You'd think that the higher a person's level of unhappi-
8 ness, the lower their level of happiness and vice versa," says
9 Edward Diener, a University of Illinois professor of psychol-
10 ogy who has done much of the new work on positive and
11 negative emotions. But when Diener and other researchers
12 measure people's average levels of happiness and unhappi-
13 ness, they often find little relationship between the two.

14   The recognition that feelings of happiness and unhap-
15 piness can coexist much like love and hate in a close rela-
16 tionship may offer valuable clues on how to lead a happier
17 life. It suggests, for example, that changing or avoiding
18 things that make you miserable may well make you less
19 miserable but probably won't make you any happier. That
20 advice is backed up by an extraordinary series of studies
21 which indicate that a genetic predisposition for unhappi-
22 ness may run in certain families. On the other hand, re-
23 searchers have found, happiness doesn't appear to be
24 anyone's heritage. The capacity for joy is a talent you de-
25 velop largely for yourself.
26   Psychologists have settled on a working definition of
27 the feeling—happiness is a sense of subjective well-being.
28 They've also begun to find out who's happy, who isn't and
29 why. To date, the research hasn't found a simple recipe for
30 a happy life, but it has discovered some of the actions and
31 attitudes that seem to bring people closer to that most de-
32 sired of feelings.
33   In a number of studies of identical and fraternal twins,
34 researchers have examined the role genetics plays in happi-
35 ness and unhappiness. The work suggests that although no
36 one is really born to be happy, sadness may run in families.
37   In one University of Southern California study, psy-
38 chologist Laura Baker and colleagues compared 899 indi-
39 viduals who had taken several commonly used tests for
40 happiness and unhappiness. The men and women in-
41 cluded 105 pairs of identical and fraternal twins as well as
42 grandparents, parents and young adult offspring from
43 more than 200 other families.
44   "Family members," Baker reports, "resembled each
45 other more in their levels of unhappiness than in their lev-
46 els of happiness." Furthermore, identical twins were much
47 closer than fraternal twins in unhappiness, a finding that
48 implies a genetic component.
49   In a study at the University of Minnesota, twins (some
50 raised together and others who had grown up apart) were
51 tested for a wide range of personality traits. In terms of
52 happiness—defined as the capacity to enjoy life—identical
53 twins who were separated soon after birth were consider-
54 ably less alike than twins raised together. But when it came
55 to *unhappiness*, the twins raised apart—some without con-
56 tact for as long as 64 years—were as similar as those who'd
57 grown up together.
58   Why is unhappiness less influenced by environment?

59 When we're happy we are more responsive to people and
60 keep up connections better than when we're feeling sad.
61   This doesn't mean, however, that some people are born
62 to be sad and that's that. Genes may predispose one to un-
63 happiness, but disposition can be influenced by personal
64 choice. You can increase your happiness through your own
65 actions.
66   In a series of experiments by psychologists John Reich
67 and Alex Zautra at Arizona State University, they asked stu-
68 dents to select their favorite activities from a list of every-
69 day pleasures—things like going to a movie, talking with
70 friends and playing cards.
71   Then the researchers instructed some of the subjects to
72 increase the number of favorite activities they participated
73 in for one month (the other participants in the study served
74 as controls and did not vary their activity level). Result:
75 Those who did more of the things they enjoyed were hap-
76 pier than those who didn't. The conclusion, then, is that the
77 pleasure we get from life is largely ours to control.

• A. Fact-Finding Exercise

Read the passage once. Then read the following statements. Scan the article quickly to find out if each statement is true (T) or false (F). If a statement is false, change it so that it is true.

_____ T _____ F   1. The feeling of unhappiness may be genetic.

_____

_____ T _____ F   2. There is a strong relationship between levels of happiness and unhappiness in a person.

_____

_____ T _____ F   3. Researchers have found that happiness is inherited.

_____

_____ T _____ F   4. Unhappiness is less influenced by environment than it is by genetics.

_____

_____ T _____ F   5. It is impossible to increase your happiness.

_____

_____ T _____ F   6. We can control our own happiness.

_____

• B. Reading Analysis

Read each question carefully. Circle the number or letter of the correct answer, or write your answer in the space provided.

1. Read lines 7 and 8: "You'd think that the higher a person's level of unhappiness, the lower their level of happiness and **vice versa**."

   a. **Vice versa** means that
      1. the lower a person's level of unhappiness, the higher their level of happiness.
      2. the higher a person's level of unhappiness, the higher their level of happiness.
      3. the lower a person's level of unhappiness, the lower their level of happiness.

   b. **Vice versa** means
      1. the same thing is true.
      2. the reverse is true.

2. Read lines 11–13. What does **the two** refer to?

   a. Diener and other researchers
   b. positive and negative emotions
   c. happiness and unhappiness

3. Read lines 17–19. **Miserable** means

   _____

4. Read lines 19–24.

   a. What does **back up** mean?
      1. go behind
      2. write
      3. support

   b. "Studies indicate that a genetic predisposition for unhappiness may run in certain families. **On the other hand**, happiness doesn't appear to be anyone's heritage." This sentence means that
      1. the tendency to be unhappy is inherited, but happiness is not.
      2. the tendency to be unhappy is inherited, and happiness is, too.
      3. the tendency to be happy is inherited, but unhappiness is not.

   c. Complete the following sentence with the appropriate choice. John is happy being a student in another country because he can study what he wants. **On the other hand,** he is unhappy because
      1. he is far from his family and friends.
      2. he knows people from many different countries.
      3. his English skills are improving.

5. Read lines 49–57.

   a. According to the University of Minnesota study, what is happiness?

      _____

   b. How do you know?

      _____

   c. Why is the phrase **some without contact for as long as 64 years** separated from the rest of the sentence by dashes (—)?

      _____

6. Read lines 61–65. **That's that** means:

    a. some people are born to be sad, and there is nothing they can do to change the situation.

    b. some people are born to be sad, and they don't think about it.

    c. some people are born to be sad, and some people are born to be happy.

7. Read lines 66–70.

    a. What are some of the everyday pleasures on the list that the students read?

    _____

    b. How do you know?

    _____

8. Read lines 74–76.

    a. **Those who didn't** refers to
      1. the students who didn't participate in the study.
      2. the students who didn't increase the number of favorite activities.
      3. the students who didn't become happier.

    b. In this context, **largely** means
      1. hugely.
      2. completely.
      3. mostly.

• C. Word Forms

Part 1

In English, verbs can change to nouns in several ways. Some verbs become nouns by adding the suffixes *-ance* or *-ence*, for example, *insist* (v.), *insistence* (n.).

Complete each sentence with the correct form of the words on the left. **Use the simple present tense of the verbs, in either the affirmative or the negative form. Use the singular form of the nouns.**

appear (v.)   1. a. Peter _____ to be very unhappy.

appearance (n.)   b. His sad _____ makes me wonder what's wrong.

avoid (v.)
avoidance (n.)

2. a. Susan always _____ going to a doctor even when she's very sick.

 b. Her _____ of doctors is not a good idea. She should see one when she's ill.

exist (v.)
existence (n.)

3. a. Some people believe in the _____ of life in other solar systems.

 b. I also think that life _____ on other planets besides Earth.

resemble (v.)
resemblance (n.)

4. a. Michael _____ his mother at all. She has blonde hair and blue eyes. He has dark hair and brown eyes.

 b. Michael has a much stronger _____ to his father, who has dark hair and eyes, too.

assist (v.)
assistance (n.)

5. a. Can you help me for a moment? I need your _____. This box is too heavy for me to pick up.

 b. If you _____ me, I won't be able to pick up the box.

perform (v.)
performance (n.)

6. a. The actor in the new play _____ very well in all his appearances.

 b. Consequently, I am looking forward to his first _____ tonight.

Part 2

In English, verbs can change to nouns in several ways. Some verbs become nouns by adding the suffixes *-ion* or *-tion*, for example, *suggest* (v.), *suggestion* (n.).

Complete each sentence with the correct form of the words on the left. Be careful of spelling changes. **Use the simple present tense of the verbs, in the affirmative form. Use the singular form of the nouns.**

indicate (v.)
indication (n.)

1. a. Traffic signals have three signals. A red light _____ "stop," and a green light means "go."

 b. A yellow, or amber, light is an _____ that the light is going to become red. It means "prepare to stop."

participate (v.)
participation (n.)

2. a. Many college students _____
in sports such as soccer, tennis, and swimming to keep in shape.

   b. In fact, regular _____ in a
sport is also a good way to make friends.

define (v.)
definition (n.)

3. a. I don't understand what *influence* means.
Can you give me a simple _____?

   b. Most people _____ *influence*
as the power to affect a person or an event.

recognize (v.)
recognition (n.)

4. a. Joan has an incredible memory for
faces. She actually _____ people
that she hasn't seen for years.

   b. Her powers of _____ are well
known among her friends.

imply (v.)
implication (n.)

5. a. Diane Swanbrow _____that
many "opposite" feelings may not really be
opposites after all.

   b. This is an interesting _____.
Are *like* and *dislike* not really opposites?

• D. Dictionary Skills

Read the dictionary entry for each word. Choose the appropriate definition. Then write the number and the synonym or meaning in the space
provided. The first one has been done as an example.

1. **recognition** *n*   **1** recognizing or being recognized: *Recognition of the
new state is unlikely*, it is unlikely that diplomatic rela-
tions will be established with it.   **2** acknowledgment.   **3** favorable attention or notice

The (*2*) *acknowledgment* that feelings of happiness and unhappiness
can coexist may offer clues to a happier life.

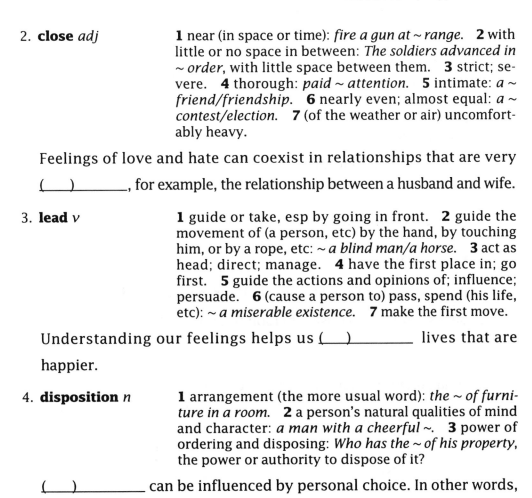

2. **close** *adj*   **1** near (in space or time): *fire a gun at ~ range.*   **2** with little or no space in between: *The soldiers advanced in ~ order,* with little space between them.   **3** strict; severe.   **4** thorough: *paid ~ attention.*   **5** intimate: *a ~ friend/friendship.*   **6** nearly even; almost equal: *a ~ contest/election.*   **7** (of the weather or air) uncomfortably heavy.

Feelings of love and hate can coexist in relationships that are very (___)_____, for example, the relationship between a husband and wife.

3. **lead** *v*   **1** guide or take, esp by going in front.   **2** guide the movement of (a person, etc) by the hand, by touching him, or by a rope, etc: *~ a blind man/a horse.*   **3** act as head; direct; manage.   **4** have the first place in; go first.   **5** guide the actions and opinions of; influence; persuade.   **6** (cause a person to) pass, spend (his life, etc): *~ a miserable existence.*   **7** make the first move.

Understanding our feelings helps us (___)_____ lives that are happier.

4. **disposition** *n*   **1** arrangement (the more usual word): *the ~ of furniture in a room.*   **2** a person's natural qualities of mind and character: *a man with a cheerful ~.*   **3** power of ordering and disposing: *Who has the ~ of his property,* the power or authority to dispose of it?

(___)_____ can be influenced by personal choice. In other words, you can increase your happiness through your own actions.

• E. Information Organization

Read the article a second time. Underline what you think are the main ideas. Then scan the article and complete the following outline, using the sentences that you have underlined to help you. You will use this outline later to answer specific questions about the article.

  I. What New Research Shows About Happiness and Unhappiness

    A. The tendency to feel unhappy may be in your genes

    B.

    C.

II. Studies on the Role of Genetics in Happiness and Unhappiness

    A. University of Southern California
       1. subjects: 899 individuals (identical and fraternal twins, grand-parents, parents, and young adult offspring)
       2. results:
       3. conclusion:

    B. University of Minnesota
       1. subjects:
       2. results:
          a. in terms of happiness,
          b. in terms of unhappiness,
       3. conclusion:

III. The Implications of the Studies on Happiness and Unhappiness

    A. Genes only predispose a person to unhappiness
    B.

IV. Arizona State University Experiment on Happiness

    A. subjects:
    B. experiment:
       1.
       2.
    C. result:
    D. conclusion: the pleasure we get from life is largely ours to control

---

• F. Information Organization Quiz and Summary

Read each question carefully. Use your notes to answer the questions. Do not refer back to the text. Write your answers in the space provided under each question. When you are finished, write a brief summary of the article.

  1. What do researchers believe about happiness and unhappiness?

_____

_____

_____

2. Describe the study done at the University of Southern California. Who did researchers study? What did the researchers learn?

_____

_____

_____

3. Describe the experiment done at Arizona State University. Who did the researchers study? How? What was the result of the study?

_____

_____

_____

4. According to this article, how can we increase our happiness?

_____

_____

_____

Summary

_____

_____

_____

_____

_____

• G. Critical Thinking Strategies

Read each question carefully. Write your response in the space provided. Remember that there is no one correct answer. Your response depends on what **you** think.

1. According to this article, feelings of happiness and unhappiness can coexist. Similarly, love and hate can coexist in a close relationship. How can you explain such conflicting feelings in a relationship? Do you think a person can be happy and sad at the same time? Explain your answer.

   _____

   _____

   _____

   _____

2. The author mentions several studies of identical and fraternal twins. These studies conclude that sadness may run in families. Why do you think researchers like to study twins rather than other brothers and sisters? Why do you think researchers compare identical twins who grew up together with identical twins who grew up apart?

   _____

   _____

   _____

   _____

3. According to the University of Southern California study, "identical twins were much closer than fraternal twins in unhappiness, a finding that implies a genetic component." Why do you think identical twins were more alike than fraternal twins were?

   _____

   _____

   _____

   _____

4. The author describes two studies, one at the University of Southern California and one at the University of Minnesota. She also describes an experiment at Arizona State University. What do you think is the difference between doing a study and doing an experiment?

_____

_____

_____

_____

5. What do you think the author believes about happiness and unhappiness? Does she believe they are opposites? What do you think her opinion is?

_____

_____

_____

_____

• H. Follow-up Discussion and Activities

1. Researchers think that sadness runs in families. Do you agree or disagree? Write a composition explaining your opinion. Give examples to support your ideas.

2. According to the author, Diane Swanbrow, there are seven steps to happiness:

   1. Develop loving relationships with other people;
   2. Work hard at what you like;
   3. Be helpful to other people;
   4. Make the time to do whatever makes you happy;
   5. Stay in good physical condition;
   6. Be organized, but be flexible in case something unexpected comes up;
   7. Try to keep things in perspective.

   Alone, or with a classmate, examine these seven steps. Put them in order of importance to you. For example, the most important step to happiness is number one; the least important step is number seven. Compare your ordered list with your classmates' lists.

3. Work with your classmates as a group.

   a. Make a list of activities that people enjoy (e.g., going to the movies, listening to music, etc.).
   b. Take a survey to see which activities each classmate enjoys. Write the results on the blackboard.
   c. Refer to the Activity Chart on page 17. Add to the chart the activities that you listed on the board. Keep a personal record of the activities you do for the rest of the term. Use each box on the right for a weekly check.
   d. At the end of the term, do an in-class survey to find out if the people who increased the number of favorite activities that they participated in actually feel happier.
   e. Do your results support or disprove the Arizona State University findings?

ACTIVITY CHART

ACTIVITY

read								
watch TV								
write letters								
listen to music								
take a walk								
go bicycling								

Hidden Disability

by Lynnie Ozer
Journal of Rehabilitation

• Prereading Preparation

1. What is a **disability**? What are some examples of different types of disabilities?
2. Look at the title. What do you think a "hidden disability" is?
3. Do you know anyone who has a disability? Describe that person. How is that person different from you? How is that person similar to you?

1 February 23rd
2   This is a special evening for me. Tomorrow I will gradu-
3 ate from New York University with a doctorate in German
4 literature—the completion of eight years of dedication. A
5 momentous occasion in anyone's life, it is a miracle in
6 mine because I was born retarded.
7   When I was sixteen months old I was diagnosed by a
8 team of doctors as a cretin dwarf. The doctors treated me
9 and after one month I was changed into a normal looking
10 infant. One of the doctors told my mother that I would
11 most likely be physically normal but that permanent men-
12 tal retardation was highly probable.
13   My parents brought me back home to New York and be-
14 gan their determined battle for my normalcy. They became
15 my therapists, making me walk when I crawled, reading to
16 me day and evening. At the age of four I began to read ev-
17 ery book I found. The mental retardation was completely
18 gone! It was fortunate that I had books and the companion-
19 ship of my parents because the neighborhood children
20 would have nothing to do with me. Despite the doctor's
21 prognosis, my physical development was severely re-
22 tarded. For example, when I was five years old I could not
23 walk without falling.

24   When I was nine, my father took a position as a rabbi in
25 a small Long Island town. I was the new girl at school. Dur-
26 ing physical education classes, the competitive girls dis-
27 covered my inability to perform like them. I became the
28 outcast for my classmates who would follow me out of the
29 locker room screaming "creep" and "freak" at me. How
30 could I have explained cretinism to them when I myself
31 didn't understand it? My condition falls into the category
32 of "hidden disability." Diabetics, epileptics and others with
33 illnesses that are not obvious are expected to be like every-
34 body else. When our illness reveals itself, it is usually not
35 understood and therefore criticized. Because there were no
36 crutches to excuse my lack of ability, my peers perceived
37 my failure as laziness.
38   When I was about eleven years old, my mother ex-
39 plained my condition to me and emphasized that the con-
40 stant rejection I experienced from my peers was not my
41 fault. Both my parents increased their efforts to be com-
42 panions to me. When it was discovered that I could sing
43 very well, I was given voice and piano lessons. By the time
44 I was in my early teens I had some status at school because
45 of the leading roles I was given in the musicals. I began to
46 dream of being a great star. My mother, with her usual re-
47 alism, discouraged my ambition. My father, however, en-
48 couraged my dreams.
49   My father deserves a great deal of credit for my survival
50 during the childhood and teen years. My mother set me on
51 the firm ground of reality, which prepared me for life's
52 hardships later on. My father gave me the wings of fantasy
53 I can put on at all times.
54   A week before I entered college my father died. During
55 the last year of his life he promised me he would always be
56 with me, and he was and is. There is no doubt that I am in-
57 debted for whatever I have achieved and overcome to my
58 courageous and loving parents.
59   When I completed my undergraduate work in singing
60 and drama with high honors, I spent seven years abroad
61 teaching, translating and singing concerts. Although my
62 performing career was only part-time, it brought me an
63 enormous sense of worth. Out of a sense of obligation to-
64 ward the medical profession which had made it possible
65 for me to lead a productive life, I took a graduate degree in
66 medical translation and worked in Munich as a translator
67 for a psychiatric research institute. When I returned to New
68 York, I found that there were no jobs for me as a teacher or

69 translator. Thus, I took a job as a bilingual administrative
70 assistant in a music publishing company. I worked hard
71 until I was promoted to the level of German Language Spe-
72 cialist. Still, I was unfulfilled creatively.

73   One evening my mother came to my apartment and
74 told me that she had the solution to my problem. She
75 would pay my tuition toward a doctorate in German litera-
76 ture. She said, "You have not had the success you wanted
77 and certainly even deserved. That is true. But you have
78 achieved something rarer than most successful people.
79 Don't ever underestimate your accomplishment in over-
80 coming your illness and all the problems in your child-
81 hood. You were privileged to triumph." Thus, my path
82 toward the goal of a doctorate began.

83   It is already eleven o'clock. I have written steadily for
84 two hours. Many people suffer far more from their disabili-
85 ties than I do. I have been fortunate. I have achieved suc-
86 cess in my life, but the gratitude I should feel at all times
87 is not always there. Will I be able to rise above these feel-
88 ings, too? I look at my father's picture and recall how he
89 loved to sing with me the freedom song "We Shall Over-
90 come." He would want me to try—at least to try.

• A. Fact-Finding Exercise

Read the passage once. Then read the following statements. Scan the article quickly to find out if each statement is true (T) or false (F). If a statement is false, change it so that it is true.

_____ T ___✗__ F   1. Lynnie Ozer is graduating today.

_____

_____ T _____ F   2. When Lynnie Ozer was a baby, the doctors believed she would have permanent mental retardation.

_____

_____ T _____ F   3. When the author was five years old, she learned to read.

_____

_____ T _____ F   4. Lynnie Ozer's classmates treated her kindly in school.

_____

_____ T _____ F   5. The author took music lessons as a child because she sang well.

_____

_____ T _____ F   6. After graduating from college, Lynnie Ozer traveled overseas.

_____

_____ T _____ F   7. Lynnie Ozer's mother encouraged her to get a doctorate in German literature.

_____

• B. Reading Analysis

Read each question carefully. Circle the number or letter of the correct answer, or write your answer in the space provided.

1. Read lines 2–4: What was the result of eight years of dedication?

   _____

2. Read lines 7–10: "When I was sixteen months old I was **diagnosed** by a team of doctors as a cretin dwarf. The doctors **treated** me and after one month I was changed into a normal looking infant."

   a. **Diagnosed** means that
      1. the doctors took care of her condition.
      2. the doctors recognized her condition.
   b. **Treated** means
      1. the doctors gave her medical care.
      2. the doctors gave her a lot of attention.

3. Read lines 18–20: "The neighborhood children would have nothing to do with me." This means that the children

   a. did not speak to her or play with her.
   b. gave her nothing.
   c. had nothing for her.

4. Read the following sentences: "One of the doctors told my mother that I would most likely be physically normal but that permanent mental retardation was highly probable. Despite the doctor's prognosis, my physical development was severely retarded. For example, when I was five years old I could not walk without falling."

   a. In this passage, which word is a synonym for **likely**?

   _____

   b. The doctor's **prognosis** was his
      1. medical help for Lynnie.
      2. prediction about Lynnie's future condition.

   c. **Despite** indicates
      1. additional information.
      2. an example.
      3. a contrast.

5. Read lines 25–29 What kind of words are "**creep**" and "**freak**"?

   a. pleasant descriptions
   b. negative names

6. Read lines 31–37.

   a. What does Lynnie Ozer mean by a "**hidden disability**"?

   _____

   b. How do you know?

   _____

   c. Who were Lynnie's **peers**?
      1. her doctors
      2. the other children
      3. her parents

7. Read lines 43–45: **Status** means

   a. respected position.
   b. good luck.
   c. popularity.

8. In line 69, what does **thus** mean?

   a. in addition
   b. as a result
   c. in contrast

9. Read lines 73 and 74. What does Lynnie Ozer mean by "my problem?"

   _____

10. In line 84, what does **far more** mean?

    a. far away
    b. for more reasons
    c. a lot more

• C. Word Forms

Part 1

In English, verbs can change to nouns in several ways. Some verbs become nouns by adding the suffix -*ment*, for example, *achieve* (v.), *achievement* (n.).

Complete each sentence with the correct form of the words on the left. **Use the simple past tense of the verbs, in either the affirmative or the negative form. Use the singular or plural form of the nouns.**

accomplish (v.)
accomplishment (n.)

1. a. Steve spent five hours in the library yesterday, but he _____ anything because he didn't study.
    b. His only _____ were that he got a few hours' sleep and read a magazine.

settle (v.)
settlement (n)

2. a. These two countries were at war for ten years before they stopped fighting and reached a _____.
    b. They finally _____ their disagreements with the help of a U.N. mediator.

develop (v.)
development (n.)

3. a. Scientists _____ an effective antibiotic until 1939.
    b. Since the 1930s, there have been many significant _____ in the field of medicine.

discourage (v.)
discouragement (n.)

4. a. When Margaret was young, she rarely experienced any _____ from the people around her.
    b. No one ever _____ her from trying anything she wanted to do. Today, she is a very happy, successful person.

enjoy (v.)
enjoyment (n.)

5. a. Last summer I really _____ going on picnics every weekend.
    b. I got so much _____ from these outings with my friends that I'm going to do it again this summer, too.

Part 2

In English, the verb and noun forms of some words are the same, for example, *influence* (v.), *influence* (n.).

Complete each sentence with the correct form of the words on the left. **Use the simple past tense of the verbs, in either the affirmative or the negative form. Use the singular or plural form of the nouns. In addition, indicate whether you are using the verb form or the noun form of the word.**

change

1. a. Linda _____ her last name
    (v., n.)
    when she got married. She kept her own name.

    b. However, she made other _____.
    (v., n.)
    She moved to a different city with her husband and got a new job.

promise

2. a. When Matt started college, he made a very
    serious _____ to himself.
    (v., n.)

    b. Matt _____ himself that he
    (v., n.)
    would graduate with honors in four years.

experience

3. a. Harry had many exciting _____
    (v., n.)
    when he went to Southeast Asia last year.

    b. In addition, he was fortunate because he
    _____ any culture shock
    (v., n.)
    while he was there.

excuse

4. a. Richard's boss is tired of all his _____
    (v., n.)
    for being late so often.

    b. She actually _____ Richard
    (v., n.)
    the first few times he was late, but she
    won't accept his latenesses any more.

estimate

5. a. Ann correctly _____ that the
    (v., n.)
    trip to the beach would take four hours.

    b. In fact, her _____ was almost
    (v., n.)
    exactly right. It took us four hours and five
    minutes to get there.

• D. Dictionary Skills

Choose the appropriate definition for each word. Then write the number and the synonym or meaning in the space provided. **Be sure to use the correct form of the verbs and nouns.**

1. **dedicate** *n*   **1** to give up, devote (one's) time, energy, etc (to a noble cause or purpose); *He ~d his life to the service of his country.*   **2** devote with solemn ceremonies (to God, to a sacred use).   **3** (of an author) write (or print) a person's name at the beginning of a book (to show gratitude or friendship to).

Lynnie Ozer had to (____)_____ for eight years in order to receive her doctorate degree.

2. **treat** *v*   **1** act or behave toward: *He ~s his wife badly.* **2** consider: *We had better ~ it as a joke,* instead of taking it seriously.   **3** discuss; deal with: *The lecturer ~ed his subject thoroughly.*   **4** give medical or surgical care to: *Which doctors are ~ing her for her illness?* **5** supply (food, drink, entertainment, etc) at one's own expense (to): *I shall ~ myself/you to a good weekend vacation.*

The doctors (____)_____ me and after one month I was transformed into a normal looking infant.

3. **transform** *v*   **1** change the shape, appearance, quality or nature of: *Success and wealth ~ed his character. A steam engine ~s heat into energy.*

The doctors treated me and after one month I was (____)_____ into a normal looking infant.

4. **overcome** *v*   **1** defeat; get the better of: *~ the enemy/a bad habit/ temptation.*   **2** exhaust; overpower: *be ~ by tiredness/ sadness/whiskey/fumes.*

There is no doubt that my parents helped me (____)_____ the physical and emotional difficulties in my life.

• E. Information Organization

Read the article a second time. Underline what you think are the main ideas. Then scan the article and complete the following table, which outlines events in Lynnie Ozer's life. You will use this table later to answer specific questions about the article. Not all the boxes will be filled in.

	What the doctors did	What Lynnie's parents did	What Lynnie did	What Lynnie's peers did
Infancy and early childhood	1. 2.	1. 2. 3.	1. 2.	1.
School years: 9 years old to 19 years old		1. 2. 3.	1. 2.	1. When Lynnie was a child: 2. As a teenager:
College years		1.	1.	
Post-College years		1.	1. 2. 3. 4. 5.	

• F. Information Organization Quiz and Summary

Read each question carefully. Use your notes to answer the questions. Do not refer back to the text. Write your answers in the space provided under each question. When you are finished, write a brief summary of the article.

1. a. What happened when Lynnie Ozer was a child?

    _____

    _____

    b. How did her parents help her?

    _____

    _____

2. a. How did Lynnie Ozer's peers treat her as a child?

    _____

    _____

    b. How did her parents react to their daughter's experiences?

    _____

    _____

3. What did Lynnie Ozer achieve as an adult?

    _____

    _____

Summary

_____

_____

_____

_____

_____

• G. Critical Thinking Strategies

Read each question carefully. Write your response in the space provided. Remember that there is no one correct answer. Your response depends on what **you** think.

1. Lynnie Ozer describes her parents' behavior after a doctor told them that Lynnie would probably have permanent mental retardation. She writes that they began a determined battle for her normalcy. They made her walk when she crawled, and read to her day and evening. What do you think Lynnie Ozer wants the reader to understand about her parents? What picture is she trying to give the reader of her parents?

_____

_____

_____

_____

2. In lines 41 and 42, Lynnie Ozer writes, "both my parents increased their efforts to be companions to me." Why do you think her parents did this?

_____

_____

_____

_____

3. Read lines 49–53. How were Lynnie Ozer's parents different in the way they treated their daughter? What are some reasons that it was necessary for them to be different?

_____

_____

_____

_____

4. In lines 54–56, Lynnie Ozer writes, "A week before I entered college my father died. During the last year of his life he promised me he would always be with me, and he was and is." What do you think Lynnie means when she says that her father was and is with her?

_____

_____

_____

_____

5. Read the final paragraph. In the last sentence, Lynnie Ozer says this about her father: "He would want me to try—at least to try." What do you think this statement tells us about Lynnie Ozer's personality? What do you think this statement tells us about her father?

_____

_____

_____

_____

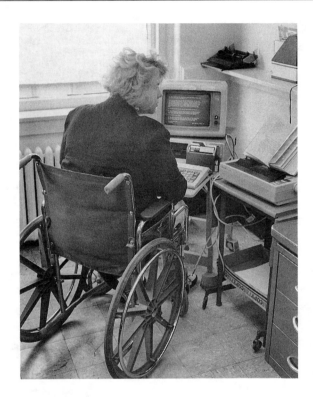

• H. Follow-up Discussion and Activities

1. Work with a partner. Make a chronological list of the events in Lynnie Ozer's life. Decide which event you believe was the most important incident in her life. Compare your answer with your other classmates' answers. Explain your reasons for your decision.
2. Think about the most important or influential events in your own life. Make a chronological list of these events. Share your list with your classmates. What are the similarities in your lists?
3. How are physically disabled people treated in your country? Do they go to special schools? Do they work, get married, have families? Explain.
4. How are mentally disabled people treated in your country? Explain.

C·H·A·P·T·E·R 3

The Birth-Order Myth

by Alfie Kohn
Health

• Prereading Preparation

1. How many brothers and sisters do you have? Are you the youngest? Are you the oldest?

2. Many people believe that birth order affects an individual's personality or intelligence. What do you think about this idea?

3. a. Write some general statements describing your classmates' personalities.

   b. Make a chart on the blackboard of how many people in the class are only children, firstborn, secondborn, thirdborn, etc.

   c. Form groups according to birth order; in other words, all the only children will form one group, all the firstborns will form one group, etc. In your groups, describe your personalities. Make a list of the personality characteristics that are common to all of you.

   d. Write the information for each group on the blackboard. Compare all the groups' responses. Discuss how these responses correspond to the descriptions of the other students in the class.

1 "No wonder he's so charming and funny—he's the baby
2 of the family!" "She works hard trying to please the boss. I
3 bet she's a firstborn." "Anyone that selfish has to be an
4 only child."
5 It's long been part of folk wisdom that birth order
6 strongly affects personality, intelligence and achievement.
7 However, most of the research claiming that firstborns are
8 radically different from other children has been discred-
9 ited, and it now seems that any effects of birth order on
10 intelligence or personality will likely be washed out by all
11 the other influences in a person's life. In fact, the belief in
12 the permanent impact of birth order, according to Toni

13 Falbo, a social psychologist at the University of Texas at
14 Austin, "comes from the psychological theory that your
15 personality is fixed by the time you're six. That assump-
16 tion simply is incorrect."
17   The better, later and larger studies are less likely to
18 find birth order a useful predictor of anything. When two
19 Swiss social scientists, Cecile Ernst and Jules Angst, re-
20 viewed 1,500 studies a few years ago, they concluded that
21 "birth-order differences in personality . . . are nonexistent
22 in our sample. In particular, there is no evidence for a
23 'firstborn personality.'"

Putting Birth Order in Context
25   Of the early studies that seemed to show birth order
26 mattered, most failed to recognize how other factors could
27 confuse the issue. Take family size: Plenty of surveys
28 showed that eldest children were overrepresented among
29 high achievers. However, that really says less about being
30 a firstborn than about not having many siblings, or any at
31 all. After all, any group of firstborns is going to include a
32 disproportionate number of children from small families,
33 since every family has a firstborn but fewer have a
34 fourthborn. Most experts now believe that position in the
35 family means little when taken out of the context of *every-
36 thing* going on in a particular household—whether sibling
37 rivalry is promoted or discouraged, for instance.
38   Parents who believe that firstborns are more capable or
39 deserving may treat them differently, thus setting up a
40 self-fulfilling prophecy.

Old Theories Die Hard
42   Consider the question of whether birth order affects
43 achievement or intelligence. Many experts today suggest
44 that birth order plays no role at all. When Judith Blake, a
45 demographer at the University of California, Los Angeles,
46 looked at birth patterns before 1938 and compared them
47 to SAT[1] scores for that group of children, she found no
48 connection. On the other hand, the *number* of siblings
49 does matter. "Small families are, on average, much more
50 supportive of the kind of verbal ability that helps people
51 succeed in school," Blake says. The reason, she believes, is
52 that parental attention is diluted in larger families.

---

[1]The Scholastic Aptitude Test; the scores on this test are used to determine high school students' ability to do college work.

53 As for effects on personality, results are mixed. Re-
54 search suggests that you're somewhat more likely to be
55 outgoing, well-adjusted and independent if you grew up
56 with few or no siblings. Two recent studies, however,
57 found no differences on the basis of size alone. The only
58 certainty is that there don't seem to be any *disadvantages*
59 to growing up in a small family—including being an only
60 child. After reviewing 141 studies in 1987, Falbo and a col-
61 league found that being raised with or without siblings
62 doesn't affect personality in predictable ways. Where small
63 differences were found—such as in achievement motiva-
64 tion—they favored the only children.

65 Do Kids Need More Space?

66 If position doesn't control destiny and family size has only
67 a minor impact, what about spacing between children? Al-
68 though little research has been conducted, some psycholo-
69 gists believe there are more advantages to having kids far
70 apart rather than close together. Some specialists caution that
71 siblings close in age may be treated as a single unit.

72 This is eyebrow-raising news, given that parents are
73 sometimes advised not to wait too long before having a
74 second child. However, different studies have led to differ-
75 ent conclusions. One found that a firstborn was more
76 likely to have high self-esteem if his or her sibling was *less*
77 than two years younger. Another indicated that spacing
78 had no impact on social competence, and others note posi-
79 tive effects for boys but not for girls.

80 As with birth order, cautions about jumping to conclu-
81 sions may be ignored by the general public. As Blake says:
82 "You're never going to completely put to rest what people
83 think is fun to believe."

• A. Fact-Finding Exercise

Read the passage once. Then read the following statements. Scan the article quickly to find out if each statement is true (T) or false (F). If a statement is false, change it so that it is true.

_____ T _____ F   1. The firstborn child in the family is different from the other children in the family.

_____

_____ T _____ F   2. Studies will probably find that birth order affects personality.

_____

_____ T _____ F   3. The number of children in a family affects personality more than birth order does.

_____

_____ T _____ F   4. Growing up in a small family has many disadvantages.

_____

_____ T _____ F   5. Many experts believe that birth order does not affect intelligence.

_____

_____ T _____ F   6. Some people believe it is better for a family to have children far apart rather than close in age.

_____

• B. Reading Analysis

Read each question carefully. Circle the number or letter of the correct answer, or write your answer in the space provided.

1. Read lines 1 and 2.

   a. What follows the dash (—)?
   1. the reason he's charming and funny

    2. extra information about him
    3. information about his family

  b. **He's the baby of the family** means
    1. he's very young.
    2. he's the youngest child.
    3. he's very immature.

2. Read the first paragraph. These statements are examples of

  a. the author's beliefs.

  b. birth-order myths.

  c. facts about birth order.

3. In lines 7–9, **discredited** means

  a. proved correct.

  b. misunderstood.

  c. found to be wrong.

4. Read lines 9–16.

  a. This statement means that, as a result of other influences, the effects of birth order
    1. will disappear.
    2. will become clean.
    3. will combine.

  b. What information follows **in fact**?
    1. true information about birth order
    2. information about Toni Falbo
    3. information to support the previous idea

  c. What word in these sentences is a synonym for **assumption**?
    1. influence
    2. belief
    3. fact

5. Read lines 18–23.

  a. What do the dots between **personality** and **are** indicate?
    1. Some words have been deleted.
    2. Both Ernst and Angst are speaking at the same time.
    3. It is a quotation.

  b. What does **in particular** mean?
    1. part of
    2. specifically
    3. in addition

6. In line 27, what does **take** mean?

   _____

7. Read lines 34–37.

   a. Why is **_everything_** in italics?

   _____

   b. The author means that
      1. sibling rivalry is important.
      2. position in the family is important.
      3. all things that are going on are important.

   c. What is the purpose of the dash (—) after **household**?
      1. to add extra information
      2. to give an example
      3. to give a definition
   d. How do you know this is the purpose of the dash?

   _____

8. Read lines 44–51.

   a. What is the SAT?

   _____

   b. How do you know?

   _____

   c. This type of information is called
      1. an abbreviation.
      2. a footnote.
      3. an asterisk.

   d. **On the other hand** indicates
      1. more information.
      2. an example.
      3. an opposing idea.

   e. Why is **_number_** in italics?

   _____

9. Read lines 53–62. **Results are mixed** means

   a. different people got different results.

   b. everyone got the same results.

   c. different people were confused about their results.

10. Read lines 66–71. **Spacing between children** means

    a. how far apart children stand.

    b. how far apart children are in age.

    c. how far apart children are from their parents.

11. Read lines 70–74. **Eyebrow-raising news** is

    a. wonderful.

    b. terrible.

    c. surprising.

• C. Word Forms

Part 1

In English, verbs can change to nouns in several ways. Some verbs become nouns by adding the suffix –*ment*, for example, *improve* (v.), *improvement* (n.).

Complete each sentence with the correct form of the words on the left. **Use the correct tense of the verbs, in either the affirmative or the negative form. Use the singular or plural form of the nouns.**

encourage (v.)   1. a. When Kevin gets married and has children,
encouragement (n.)   he _____ them to work hard.

                                     b. Kevin believes that strong parental
                                          _____ makes children successful.

achieve (v.)   2. a. Most big _____ result from
achievement (n.)   hard work.

                                       b. We may not always be successful, but surely
                                        we _____ anything if we don't try.

improve (v.)   3. a. The mayor plans to make significant
improvement (n.)   _____ to all the city parks.

                                       b. First, the mayor _____ the
                                       tennis courts and baseball fields. Then, she
                                       will put in new park benches.

state (v.)   4. a. This morning the president _____
statement (n.)   that he would not run for reelection.

                                       b. He made this surprising _____
                                       at a news conference in Washington, D.C.

treat (v.)   5. a. Doctors usually _____ infections with
treatment (n.)   antibiotics such as penicillin.

                                       b. A severe infection may require several
                                       _____ over a long period of time.

Part 2

In English, some adjectives become nouns by deleting a final -*t* and adding -*ce*, for example, *important* (adj.), *importance* (n.).

Complete each sentence with the correct form of the words on the left.

competent (adj.)

competence (n.)

1. a. Winifred is an extremely _____ businesswoman.
   b. After working at a firm for only a few years, she developed enough _____ to start her own business, which has become very successful.

intelligent (adj.)

intelligence (n.)

2. a. It is impossible to measure _____ on a test because people have different kinds of aptitudes.
   b. Besides, even a very _____ person can become nervous and do poorly on a test.

permanent (adj.)

permanence (n.)

3. a. Peter has never had a really _____ home.
   b. Peter's parents have always moved from one city to another every few years, so the idea of _____ is something very strange to him.

significant (adj.)

significance (n.)

4. a. There has been a _____ decrease in the population of this city in the last ten years.
   b. The _____ of this population decline in schools is that there tend to be fewer students in each class.

different (adj.)

difference (n.)

5. a. I can't taste any _____ between regular coffee and decaffeinated coffee.
   b. However, I drink them at _____ times of the day. For instance, I drink regular coffee in the morning, but I drink decaffeinated coffee in the evening.

• D. Dictionary Skills

Indicate the number of the definition for each word. Then write the synonym or meaning in the space provided. **Be sure to use the correct form of the verbs and nouns**.

1. **radical** *adj*   **1** of or from the root; fundamental: ~ *changes*. **2** (*esp politics*) favoring complete and drastic changes.

People no longer believe that there is a (____)_____ difference between firstborn children and other children.

2. **claim** *v*   **1** demand recognition of the fact that one is, or owns, or has a right to (something): *He ~ed to be the owner of/~ed that he owned the land.* **2** say that something is a fact: *He ~ed to be the best tennis player in the school.* **3** (of things) need; deserve: *There are several matters that ~ my attention.*

People no longer (____)_____ that there is a radical difference between firstborn children and other children.

3. **fix** *v*   **1** make firm or fast; fasten (something) so that it cannot be moved: *~ shelves to a wall.* **2** (of objects) attract and hold (the attention): *This unusual sight kept his attention ~ed.* **3** set; determine or decide: *~ the rent/a date for a meeting; ~ed the blame.* **4** mend; repair: *They've ~ed all the broken windows.* **5** put in order; prepare: *~ one's hair,* brush and comb it.

The assumption that heredity and our environment (____)_____ our personality by the time we're six is incorrect.

4. **promote** *v*   **1** give (a person) higher position or rank: *He was ~ed sergeant/to the rank of sergeant.* **2** help to organize and start; help the progress of: *try to ~ good feelings (between . . .).*

Some parents (____)_____ sibling rivalry among their children.

• E. Information Organization

Read the article a second time. Underline what you think are the main ideas. Then scan the article and complete the following outline, using the sentences that you have underlined to help you. You will use this outline later to answer specific questions about the article.

I. The Myth and the Reality About Birth Order

    A. The Myth:

    B. The Reality:

II.

    A. The findings of Cecile Ernst and Jules Angst
       1. Birth-order differences in personality are nonexistent
       2.

    B.
       1. Birth order does not affect intelligence; she looked at birth patterns before 1938 and compared them to SAT scores for that group of children, and she found no connection

III.

    A.
       1. It does affect intelligence; small families tend to be more supportive of the kind of verbal ability that helps people succeed in school

    B.
       1. Parents who believe that firstborns are more capable or deserving may treat them differently, thus setting up a self-fulfilling prophecy

    C.
       1. Some psychologists believe there are more advantages to having kids far apart
       2. One study found that a firstborn was more likely to have high self-esteem if his or her sibling was *less* than two years younger

IV.

    A. You're more likely to be outgoing, well adjusted, and independent if you grew up with few or no siblings

    B.

    C. One study indicated that spacing had no impact on social competence

• F. Information Organization Quiz and Summary

Read each question carefully. Use your notes to answer the questions. Do not refer back to the text. Write your answers in the space provided under each question. When you are finished, write a brief summary of the article.

1. a. What do many people believe about birth order?

   _____

   _____

   b. What is the truth about birth order?

   _____

   _____

2. What were the research results about birth order?

   _____

   _____

3. What are three family factors that may have more effect on personality and intelligence than birth order? Explain each one.

   a. _____

   _____

   _____

   b. _____

   _____

   _____

   c. _____

   _____

   _____

4. Were all the results of research about family size and birth order the same?

   _____

   _____

Summary

_____

_____

_____

_____

_____

_____

_____

_____

• G. Critical Thinking Strategies

Read each question carefully. Write your response in the space provided. Remember that there is no one correct answer. Your response depends on what **you** think.

1. The author writes, "Parents who believe that firstborns are more capable or deserving may treat them differently, thus setting up a self-fulfilling prophecy." The self-fulfilling prophecy is that children live up to their parents' expectations. How do you think parents influence their children by treating them differently?

   _____

   _____

   _____

   _____

2. According to the article, the number of siblings a person has affects his or her personality. As Judith Blake says, "Small families are, on average, much more supportive of the kind of verbal ability that helps people succeed in school." The reason, she believes, is that parental attention is diluted in larger families. Why do you think parental attention might be diluted in larger families? Do you agree with this theory? Explain your answer.

   _____

   _____

   _____

   _____

3. One study found that a firstborn was more likely to have high self-esteem if his or her sibling was *less* than two years younger. Another indicated that spacing had no impact on social competence, and others note positive effects for boys but not for girls. What conclusion can you make about these different studies?

_____

_____

_____

_____

4. The studies that the author refers to in this article came up with very different results. How do you think we might explain these different findings?

_____

_____

_____

_____

5. Read the last paragraph cf the article. What does Judith Blake mean? Why may people ignore the findings about the birth-order myth?

_____

_____

_____

_____

6. What do you think the author's opinion about birth order is? Why do you think so?

_____

_____

_____

_____

• H. Follow-up Discussion and Activities

1. What stereotypes do you have in your country about children and birth order? How do you think these myths came about?

2. What do you think are the advantages and disadvantages of being an only child? Write a composition explaining your opinion. Indicate if you are an only child, or whether or not you would like to be an only child.

3. a. Refer to the Birth Order Survey on page 48. As a class, add more pairs of adjectives to complete the survey.

   b. After you have finished the questionnaire, go outside your class alone or in pairs. Survey two or three people. Then bring back your data and combine it with the other students' information. How do your results compare with the results you obtained in your class? Do you think the idea of birth-order characteristics is convincing, or is it a myth?

4. Think about your in-class and questionnaire findings and the article you have just read.

   a. What was your opinion about birth-order myths before you did your surveys and read this article? Do you still have that opinion?

   b. Does the information you collected support the author's findings or conflict with them? Give reasons for your answer.

Birth-Order Survey

The purpose of this questionnaire is to collect data regarding birth order. Please answer the following questions.

1. Do you have siblings? How many?

   _____

2. What is your order of birth? That is, are you an only child, firstborn, secondborn, thirdborn? *Are you also the youngest child?*

   _____

3. Please indicate one of each of the pairs of adjectives that describes your personality.

1. anxious/confident	13. mature/immature
2. patient/impatient	14. funny/serious
3. boring/interesting	15.
4. talkative/quiet	16.
5. understanding/insensitive	17.
6. diligent/lazy	18.
7. friendly/disagreeable	19.
8. competitive/cooperative	20.
9. considerate/thoughtless	21.
10. creative/unimaginative	22.
11. curious/indifferent	23.
12. dependent/independent	24.

Unit I Review

• I. Vocabulary Categorization

The words in the vocabulary list below have been taken from the three readings in this unit. Read through the list, and place the words into the three categories indicated. For example, *happiness* belongs in the category of feelings and emotions. Some words may belong to more than one category.

ability	enjoyment	retardation
achievement	experiment	self-esteem
ambition	failure	selfishness
competition	genetics	talent
dedication	gratitude	treatment
diagnosis	heredity	triumph
disability	independence	unfulfillment
discouragement	misery	unhappiness
disease	motivation	well-being
encouragement	prognosis	wisdom

ACHIEVEMENT/SUCCESS   **HEALTH/MEDICINE**   **FEELINGS/EMOTIONS**

happiness

• J. Crossword Puzzle

Across

5. Competition between people
8. A _____ is something that seems untrue, but is true.
9. Brothers and sisters
12. The opposite of **yes**
16. I am going ____ work.
17. Vary
18. A person's standing or position
19. Feelings, such as happiness, anger, joy, fear
23. Children
25. This, _____, these, those
26. Lucky
29. Surroundings; everything around you
31. _____, two, three
33. A statement that is accepted as true without proof; a supposition

Down

1. Encourage
2. The opposite of **under**
3. A special advantage; a benefit
4. People of equal standing; your classmates or colleagues, for example
6. This is the ___ book she wrote. She wrote this one book.
7. Sickness; disease
10. The answer to a problem
11. Difficulties
13. In a university, a student first gets a bachelor's degree, then a master's degree, then a ___.
14. The past of **hit**
15. Exist together; exist at the same time
20. Clues; indications
21. The opposite of **bottom**
22. Twins can be either identical or _____
24. Quit; cease
27. _____, she, it
28. The past of **is**
30. The past of **run**
32. I _____ a student.

• K. Unit I Discussion

1. The articles in Unit I all relate to what influences our satisfaction. Discuss what factors in our lives we can control or change, e.g., happiness, and those we cannot, e.g., birth order. Which factors do you think are most important towards achieving satisfaction? Why? Explain your reasons.

2. a. Lynnie Ozer is an only child. Do you think she fits the description of an only child as you discussed it in Chapter 3? Explain your answer.

   b. How do you think Lynnie Ozer's life might have been different if she had had brothers and sisters?

3. When parents have a disabled child, they sometimes decide not to have any more children. They feel that they need to focus their energy on taking care of the disabled child, who needs more care than a normal child. What do you think about this idea? How do you think it affects a disabled child who is also the youngest in the family?

• Library Resource Mastery

Introduction

Information is stored in the library in both books and periodicals.

Some material in the library may be taken out, or borrowed, for a specific period of time. Other material may be used only in the library. This material is usually reference work. However, it is usually possible to photocopy whatever you need because most American libraries have photocopying facilities.

In all libraries, the books are kept on shelves, called stacks. The stacks may be *open*; that is, the users have access to the bookshelves. Some libraries have *closed* stacks. In this case, the user presents a request to a library assistant and the assistant goes into the stacks to get the book.

Using the Card Catalog

The card catalog has three cards for each book in the library: a title card, an author card, and a subject card. Because this book is a biography, the title card and the subject card are the same.

1. What information is on both cards?

_____

_____

Title Card/Subject Card

CURIE, MARIE SKLODOWSKA, 1867–1934

QD   Reid, Robert William.
22   Marie Curie [by] Robert Reid. New York
C8   Saturday Review Press [1974]
R4   349 p. illus.
1974

Bibliography: p. 337–338

1. Curie, Marie Sklodowska, 1867–1934
I. Title

Author Card

Reid, Robert William

QD
22
C8   Reid, Robert William.
R4   Marie Curie [by] Robert Reid. New York
1974   Saturday Review Press [1974]
                    349 p. illus.

Bibliography: p. 337–338

1. Curie, Marie Sklodowska, 1867–1934
I. Title

2. a. What information is on the first line of the title card?

_____

b. What information is on the first line of the author card?

_____

The card catalog may be a set of cabinets full of index cards, or it may be computerized. If it is computerized, there will be specific, simple instructions on how to use the system. Some libraries have both setups.

1. What system is currently in use at your school or local library?

_____

Call Numbers

Call numbers are a system of numbers and letters used to identify every book in the library. Libraries in the United States use the Library of Congress system, although many older books are still cataloged under the outdated Dewey Decimal system. All the books on a particular subject have the same *call letter(s).*

1 a. Where do you think all the books on a single subject are located in the stacks: in the same place or in different places? Why?

_____

b. Why is this more advantageous than having all the books in the library in alphabetical order by author?

_____

_____

Library of Congress Classification

A   General Works
B-BJ   Philosophy, Psychology, Religion
C-E   History
F   History: America (Western Hemisphere)
G   Geography, Maps, Anthropology, Recreation
H   Social Sciences
J   Political Science
K   Law
L   Education
M   Music
N   Fine Arts
P   Language and Literature

Q Science
R Medicine
S Agriculture
T Technology
U Military Science
V Naval Science
Z Bibliography, Library Science

Dewey Decimal System

000 Generalities
100 Philosophy
200 Religion
300 Social Sciences
400 Language
500 Pure Sciences
600 Technology
700 The Arts
800 Literature
900 Geography and History

Library Assignment

1. Go to the library. Use the card catalog to locate a book about a famous person you are interested in. Look through the book. Find out the person's birth order and some of his or her personality characteristics. Report back to the class.

2. a. In class, use the blackboard to list by birth order the famous people each student researched.

   b. Next to each person, write a few of that person's personality characteristics.

   c. Examine the characteristics of the people who have the same birth order. Decide whether your information supports the birth order stereotypes described in the article you have just read.

Safety and Health

Why So Many More Americans Die in Fires

by Donald G. McNeil, Jr.
The New York Times

• Prereading Preparation

1. What are some ways that fires start?
2. What are some things that we can do to prevent fires?
3. Are there many fires in your city?
4. If someone has a fire in his or her home in your country, how will the neighbors react?
5. If someone has a fire in his or her home in the United States, how do you think the neighbors will react?
6. Do you think all fires are accidental?
7. Look at the title. What do you think this article will be about?

1   In some ways, the United States has made spectacular
2 progress. Fires no longer destroy 18,000 buildings as they
3 did in the Great Chicago Fire of 1871, or kill half a town of
4 2,400 people, as they did the same night in Peshtigo, Wis-
5 consin. Other than the Beverly Hills Supper Club fire in
6 Kentucky in 1977, it has been four decades since more
7 than 100 Americans died in a fire.
8   But even with such successes, the United States still has
9 one of the worst fire death rates in the world—worse than
10 all of western Europe and Asia. Safety experts say the prob-
11 lem is neither money nor technology, but the indifference
12 of a country that just will not take fires seriously enough.
13   American fire departments are some of the world's fast-
14 est and best-equipped. They have to be. The United States
15 has twice Japan's population, and 40 times as many fires.
16 It spends far less on preventing fires than on fighting
17 them. And American fire-safety lessons are aimed almost
18 entirely at children, who die in disproportionately large

19 numbers in fires but who, contrary to popular myth, start
20 very few of them.
21   Experts say the fatal error is an attitude that fires are
22 not really anyone's fault. That is not so in other countries,
23 where both public education and the law treat fires as ei-
24 ther a personal failing or a crime. Japan has many wood
25 houses; of the estimated 48 fires in world history that
26 burned more than 10,000 buildings, Japan has had 27.
27 Penalties for causing a severe fire by negligence can be as
28 high as life imprisonment. Have a simple house fire, and
29 "your neighbors may ask you to move away," said Mr.
30 Schaenman, whose Tridata Corporation of Arlington, Va.,
31 analyzes other countries' fire-safety programs. Officials
32 with loudspeakers address crowds at fires, embarrassing
33 those responsible and preaching fire safety.
34   Most European countries have tougher building codes
35 and insurance laws. In the Netherlands, every room must
36 have two exits. In France, to deter landlord arson, insurers
37 are not allowed to repay the full cost of damage. In Swit-
38 zerland, they pay only if an identical structure is rebuilt.
39   Public education is also better in Asia and Europe. Korea
40 holds neighborhood fire drills. Hong Kong apartment build-
41 ings have fire marshals. The Japanese learn to use extinguish-
42 ers at work. In England, the London Fire Brigade spends
43 roughly $1 million a year on fire-safety commercials.
44   In the United States, most education dollars are spent
45 in elementary schools. But the lessons are aimed at too
46 limited an audience; just 9 percent of all fire deaths are
47 caused by children playing with matches.
48   Adults are the ones who leave the pans on the stove,
49 smoke in bed, overload house wiring and buy unsafe heat-
50 ers. Adults fail to buy fire extinguishers, remove smoke-
51 detector batteries and do dangerous things like throw
52 water into pots of flaming French fries.
53   The United States continues to rely more on technology
54 than laws or social pressure. There are smoke detectors in
55 85 percent of all homes. Some local building codes now
56 require home sprinklers. New heaters and irons shut them-
57 selves off if they are tipped. Eventually, new stoves will
58 turn themselves off if left on too long.
59   A handful of towns are fining people who have serious
60 fires because they let smoke detectors go dead, said John
61 Ottoson, a senior analyst with the U.S. Fire Administration.
62 He knew of one landlord who was charged with man-

63 slaughter when tenants were killed. But without more such
64 changes in perception the United States seems unlikely to
65 close the gap between the rate of fire fatalities in the
66 United States and other countries.

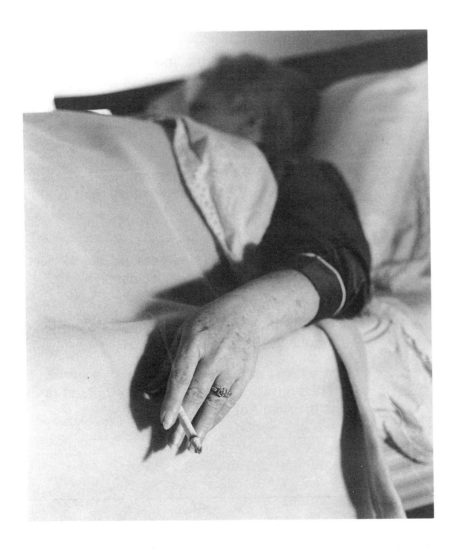

• A. Fact-Finding Exercise

Read the passage once. Then read the following statements. Scan the article quickly to find out if each statement is true (T) or false (F). If a statement is false, change it so that it is true.

_____ T _____ F   1. The fire death rate in the United States is worse than those of Western Europe and Asia.

_____

_____ T _____ F   2. The United States has more fires than Japan.

_____

_____ T _____ F   3. Children start most of the fires that occur in the United States.

_____

_____ T _____ F   4. Japan has had more than half of the fires in world history that burned more than 10,000 buildings.

_____

_____ T _____ F   5. In the Netherlands, insurers are not allowed to repay the full cost of fire damage.

_____

_____ T _____ F   6. Most homes in the United States do not have smoke detectors.

_____

_____ T _____ F   7. The high fire death rate in the United States is the result of bad technology.

_____

• B. Reading Analysis

Read each question carefully. Circle the number or letter of the correct answer, or write your answer in the space provided.

1. In line 2 and in line 4, what does **they** refer to?

   a. people

   b. buildings

   c. fires

2. a. In line 4, what is **Peshtigo**?

   _____

   b. In lines 4–5, what is **Wisconsin**?

   _____

3. In line 6, how much time is four decades?

   a. 4 years

   b. 40 years

   c. 400 years

4. Read lines 5–7. How many people died in the Beverly Hills Supper Club fire?

   a. more than 100 people

   b. fewer than 100 people

5. a. Read lines 13–15. What does **they have to be** mean?

   _____

   _____

   b. What is the purpose of this sentence?
      1. explanation
      2. emphasis
      3. contrast

6. Read lines 21–24. What does **That is not so in other countries** mean?

   _____

   _____

7. Read lines 36 and 37.

   a. What does **deter** mean?
      1. punish
      2. cause
      3. prevent

   b. What does **arson** mean?
      1. to start a fire accidentally
      2. to start a fire deliberately

   c. What is a **landlord**?
      1. a person who owns a building
      2. a person who rents a place to live

8. In line 57, what does **eventually** refer to?

   a. right now

   b. in the future

   c. recently

9. Read lines 59–61.

   a. What does **handful** mean?
     1. a large number
     2. a small number

   b. **Fining** people means
     1. putting people in jail.
     2. making people leave town.
     3. charging people money.

10. Read lines 62–63.

   a. What are **tenants**?
     1. people who rent apartments
     2. people who own apartments
     3. people who start fires

   b. What happened to the tenants?
     1. They went to jail.
     2. They moved.
     3. They died.

   c. What does **manslaughter** mean?
     1. robbery
     2. arson
     3. murder

11. Read lines 63–66.

   a. **The United States seems unlikely to close the gap** means
     1. the United States will probably close the gap.
     2. the United States probably won't close the gap.

   b. A **gap** is a
     1. space.
     2. number.
     3. difference.

   c. What does **fatalities** mean?
     1. deaths
     2. injuries
     3. damages

• C. Word Forms

Part 1

In English, some adjectives become nouns by deleting the final -*t* and adding -*ce*, for example, *independent* (adj.), *independence* (n.)
    Complete each sentence with the correct form of the words on the left.

important (adj.)
importance (n.)

1. a. It is extremely _____ to keep fresh batteries in your smoke detector.
   b. I cannot overemphasize the vital _____ of this practice—it could save your life one day.

negligent (adj.)
negligence (n.)

2. a. Mr. and Mrs. O'Hara were accused of criminal _____ when their house caught fire while their children were home alone.
   b. They had also been quite _____ about keeping matches away from their children; in fact, that's how the fire started.

dependent (adj.)
dependence (n.)

3. a. Most city people have more _____ on public transportation than they do on cars.
   b. They tend to be so _____ on trains and buses because street traffic is usually very heavy.

indifferent (adj.)
indifference (n.)

4. a. Chris shows such _____ to his classes that I'm afraid he's going to fail them.
   b. He's not only _____ to his courses; he doesn't care about his job, either.

excellent (adj.)
excellence (n.)

5. a. This particular model of car is an _____ automobile.
   b. In fact, it has won an award for _____ three years in a row.

Part 2

In English, some adjectives become nouns by adding the suffix *-ity*, for example, *equal* (adj.), *equality* (n.).

Complete each sentence with the correct form of the words on the left. **Use the singular or plural form of the nouns.**

fatal (adj.)   1. a. Yesterday, Tony saw a _____ accident
fatality (n.)   on the highway.

                       b. A car collided with a truck; there were sev-
                           eral _____.

public (adj.)   2. a. Most film actors enjoy being in the
publicity (n.)   _____ eye.

                       b. In other words, they like getting a lot of
                           _____ from the press.

safe (adj.)   3. a. Many jobs that are considered _____
safety (n.)   today used to be very dangerous.

                       b. The reason these jobs are less hazardous
                           now is because laws have been passed to
                           ensure the reasonable _____ of
                           employees.

responsible (adj.)   4. a. Parents have serious _____ toward
responsibility (n.)   their children.

                       b. For instance, parents are unquestionably
                           _____ for their children's safety,
                           health, education, and socialization.

possible (adj.)   5. a. When we worked on the math problem,
possibility (n.)   we realized that there were several
                               _____ solutions.

                       b. Of all the _____, however, we chose
                           the simplest explanation because it was the
                           clearest.

• D. Dictionary Skills

Choose the appropriate definition for each word. Then write the number and synonym or meaning in the space provided. **Be sure to use the correct form of the verbs and nouns**.

1. **negligence** *n*   **1** carelessness; failure to take proper care or precautions: *The accident was due to ~.*   **2** a negligent act.

   Penalties for causing a severe fire by (___)_____can be as high

   as life imprisonment.

2. **address** *v*   **1** make a speech to: *Mr. Green will now ~ the meeting.* **2** speak to, using a title: *Don't ~ me as "Colonel"; I'm only a major.*   **3** write the name and address on a letter, etc.

   Officials with loudspeakers (___)_____ crowds at fires, preaching

   fire safety.

3. **marshall** *n*   **1** officer of the highest rank in the military forces of some countries.   **2** official in charge of important public events or ceremonies: *grand ~ of the parade.*   **3** federal official with functions similar to those of a sheriff.   **4** head of a fire or police department in some U.S. cities.

   Hong Kong apartment buildings have fire (___)_____who help

   people get out of a burning building safely.

4. **pressure** *n*   **1** pressing.   **2** (amount of) force exerted on or against something: *air ~.*   **3** force or influence: *The union put ~ on him to vote for the bill.*   **4** something that is difficult to bear: *the ~ of taxation.*

   The United States continues to rely more on technology than on laws

   or social (___)_____.

• E. Information Organization

Read the article a second time. Underline what you think are the main ideas. Then scan the article and complete the following table, using the sentences that you have underlined to help you. You will use this table later to answer specific questions about the article. Not all the boxes will be filled in.

	The United States	Europe	Asia
People's attitudes towards fires	1. People:	1. Public education and the law:	1. Public education and the law:
How countries deal with fires	1.American fire departments: 2.	1. In the Netherlands: 2. In France: 3. In Switzerland:	In Japan: 1. 2. 3.
Public education	1. Fire-safety lessons:	1. In England:	1. Korea: 2. Hong Kong: 3. Japan:
Technology for fire prevention	1. 2. 3. 4.		
How attitudes towards fires are changing	1. 2.		

• F. Information Organization Quiz and Summary

Read each question carefully. Use your notes to answer the questions. Do not refer back to the text. Write your answers in the space provided under each question. When you are finished, write a brief summary of the article.

1. What is the difference in attitudes toward fires between Americans and people in other countries?

   _____

   _____

   _____

2. In general, what is the difference between how fires are dealt with in Asia and in Western Europe and how they are dealt with in the United States?

   _____

   _____

   _____

3. Is public education about fire safety different in the United States from public education in Asia and Europe? Why, or why not?

   _____

   _____

   _____

4. How are Americans' attitudes toward fire changing?

   _____

   _____

   _____

Summary

_____

_____

_____

_____

_____

• G. Critical Thinking Strategies

Read each question carefully. Write your response in the space provided. Remember that there is no one correct answer. Your response depends on what **you** think.

1. Read the first paragraph. How does the author feel that the United States has made progress?

   _____

   _____

   _____

   _____

2. In lines 14 and 15, the author states, "The United States has twice Japan's population, and 40 times as many fires." What do you think this information implies?

   _____

   _____

   _____

   _____

3. Read lines 16–19.

   a. What does the author think of the United States' fire-prevention methods?

   _____

   _____

   _____

   _____

   b. What does the author think the United States should do to lower its fire death rate?

   _____

   _____

   _____

   _____

4. Read lines 25–30. According to this article, if you had a house fire in Japan, why might your neighbors ask you to move away?

_____

_____

_____

_____

5. Read lines 35–38. What do insurers think some landlords might do to their property? Why do you think they might do this?

_____

_____

_____

_____

6. Read lines 59–63. How do you think these two examples show a change in Americans' attitudes toward fires?

_____

_____

_____

_____

• H. Follow-up Discussion and Activities

1. What are people's attitudes toward fires in your country? How are these attitudes similar to those in the United States? How are they different? Write a composition expressing your ideas about this.

2. a. Read the following list of fires. Which fires were caused by negligence?

   1. Harry fell asleep while he was smoking in bed, and his house burned down.
   2. Lightning struck a house, which burned to the ground.
   3. Regina was frying chicken. When the fat caught fire, she tried to put the fire out with water, and the fire spread to the entire kitchen.
   4. The wind blew down an electrical power line and set fire to a store.

   b. Think about the fires that were caused by negligence. How could these fires have been prevented?

3. Work in pairs or small groups. The owners of an apartment building have asked you to make a list of building codes for the new
   building they are planning to construct.

4. Work in pairs or small groups. You are on a committee whose job
   is to create tougher fire laws for your city.

5. Work with a partner. Make a list of things you should not do that
   could cause a fire at home.

6. Work with a partner. Make a list of things you can do at home to
   prevent a fire.

• Library Resource Mastery

Every library includes a Reference area. This section includes dictionaries, almanacs, atlases, and encyclopedias. These materials may be used only in the library; they cannot be taken out.

• Library Assignment

1. a. Go to the reference section of the library. Ask the librarian where the almanac is located.

   b. Use the almanac to find out about the worst fire in history. Where was it? When did it occur? How much damage did it cause? How many people were killed?

   c. What was the worst fire in your country or area of the world? When did it take place? Where did it occur? How many people were killed? How much damage did it cause?

   d. Report your findings to the class. Compare the fires you researched.

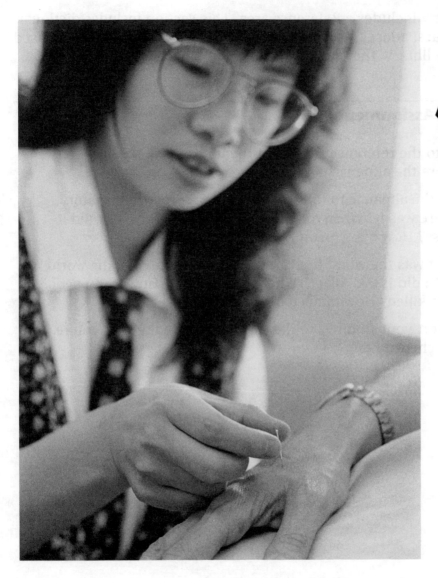

Acupuncture: The New Old Medicine

Edited by William G. Flanagan
Forbes

• Prereading Preparation

1. What do you know about **acupuncture**? How is it done? Is it a new kind of medicine?
2. Why do people get acupuncture treatments?
3. Have you ever had acupuncture treatments, or do you know someone who has? Describe the experience and the reason for the treatment.
4. Acupuncture is a traditional form of medicine. Do you know of some other traditional kinds of medicine? Are these treatments different from more "modern" medical treatments? How?
5. Read the title of this chapter. Why is acupuncture called the "new old medicine"?

1   The thin, extremely sharp needles didn't hurt at all go-
2 ing in. Dr. Gong pricked them into my left arm, around the
3 elbow that had been bothering me. Other needles were
4 slipped into my left wrist and, strangely, my *right* arm, and
5 then into both my closed eyelids.
6   There wasn't any discomfort, just a mild warming sen-
7 sation, when the electrodes were connected to the needles
8 in my left arm, and my muscles began to twitch involun-
9 tarily. However, I did begin to wonder what had driven me
10 here, to the office of Dr. James Gong, a floor up from Mott
11 Street in New York's Chinatown.
12   Then I remembered—the excruciating pain in that left
13 elbow. Several trips to a Fifth Avenue neurologist and two
14 expensive, uncomfortable medical tests had failed to pro-
15 duce even a diagnosis. "Maybe you lean on your left arm
16 too much," the neurologist concluded, suggesting I see a
17 bone doctor.

18   During the hours spent waiting in vain to see an ortho-
19 pedist, I decided to take another track and try acupunc-
20 ture. A Chinese-American friend recommended Dr. Gong. I
21 took the subway to Canal Street and walked past the open-
22 air fish stalls, the incense shops, the Asia Bank branch and
23 restaurants with cooked ducks hanging in their windows.
24 Reaching Gong's second-floor office, marked with a hand-
25 painted sign, I felt I could have been in old Hong Kong.

26   Dr. Gong speaks English, but not often. Most of my
27 questions to him were greeted with a friendly laugh, but I
28 managed to let him know where my arm hurt. He hustled
29 me into a room, had me lie down on a cot, and went to
30 work. In the next room, I learned, a woman dancer was also
31 getting a treatment. As I lay there a while, becoming oblivi-
32 ous to the needles and the muscle spasms and the electric
33 current shooting through my arm, I drifted into a dream-
34 like state and fantasized about what she looked like.

35   Not every acupuncturist offers such fantasy trips to
36 China and beyond along with the price of treatment, of
37 course. Acupuncturists today are as likely to be found on
38 Park Avenue as on Mott Street, and they are as likely to be
39 Caucasian as Asian. In all there are an estimated 10,000
40 acupuncturists in the country, 6,500 of whom are certified
41 one way or another. Nowadays, a lot of M.D.s have learned
42 acupuncture techniques; so have a number of dentists.
43 Reason? Patient demand. Few, though, can adequately ex-
44 plain how acupuncture works.

45   Acupuncturists may say that the body has more than
46 800 acupuncture points. A life force called *qi* (pronounced
47 CHEE) circulates through the body. Points on the skin are
48 energetically connected to specific organs, body structures
49 and systems. Acupuncture points are stimulated to bal-
50 ance the circulation of *qi*. It's all very confusing.

51   The truth is, though acupuncture is at least 2,200 years
52 old, "nobody really knows what's happening," says Paul
53 Zmiewski, a Ph.D. in Chinese studies who practices acu-
54 puncture in Philadelphia.

55   Millions of Americans now seek out the services of acu-
56 puncturists, usually because conventional medicine failed
57 to cure their ills. Jack Tymann, 51, president and general
58 manager of Westinghouse Electronic Systems Co., is typi-
59 cal. Tymann was bothered for 15 years with severe lower
60 back pain. His doctor suggested disc surgery, but he de-
61 cided to try acupuncture instead.

62 A scientist and an engineer by education, Tymann was
63 highly skeptical at first. "I went in with that symptom, and
64 haven't had any trouble with my back since," he says. He
65 still goes for treatments, four or five times per year—not
66 for back pain, but as a preventive measure. "It's been my
67 primary form of health care for about nine years now," he
68 says.

69 Harwood Beville, 51, executive vice president of the
70 Rouse Co., started acupuncture nine years ago, for treat-
71 ment of "what I'll call tennis shoulder." The shoulder had
72 bothered him for two years, and visits to other doctors met
73 with no success. Acupuncture had worked for his wife. Af-
74 ter a few treatments, his pain was gone, and there were
75 other noticeable effects. "Immediately, stress didn't seem
76 to be bothering me so much." Like Tymann, he, too, still
77 goes for regular treatments.

78 Acupuncture is used to treat a variety of ailments—anxi-
79 ety, depression, back pain, smoking, high blood pressure,
80 stress, arthritis; the list goes on. Acupuncture is even used
81 to help treat drug addiction—with considerable success.

82 The number of treatments can vary, although one-shot
83 cures are relatively rare. It usually takes four to six ses-
84 sions to treat a specific ailment. If that doesn't work, you
85 will probably feel at least somewhat better. After five treat-
86 ments from Dr. Gong, there has been dramatic improve-
87 ment in my arm, and the pain is a fraction of what it was. I
88 feel less stress, too. I think. The mainly silent Dr. Gong fi-
89 nally even offered a diagnosis for what ailed me. "Pinched
90 nerve," he said.

• A. Fact-Finding Exercise

Read the passage once. Then read the following statements. Scan the article quickly to find out if each statement is true (T) or false (F). If a statement is false, change it so that it is true.

_____ T _____ F   1. Dr. Gong is a neurologist.

_____

_____ T _____ F   2. The neurologist was not able to stop the author's pain.

_____

_____ T _____ F   3. Dr. Gong's office is on Fifth Avenue.

_____

_____ T _____ F   4. Dr. Gong does not know how to speak English.

_____

_____ T _____ F   5. It is hard to explain how acupuncture works.

_____

_____ T _____ F   6. Jack Tymann continues to visit an acupuncturist because his back still hurts.

_____

_____ T _____ F   7. Most acupuncture treatments take more than one session.

_____

• B. Reading Analysis

Read each question carefully. Circle the number or letter of the correct answer, or write your answer in the space provided.

1. In the first paragraph, what is a synonym for **pricked into**?

   _____

2. In lines 9–11, the author writes, "However, I did begin to wonder **what had driven me** to Dr. Gong's office." This means that the author was thinking about

   a. how he had gotten there.

   b. why he had gone there.

   c. what Dr. Gong does.

3. Read lines 13–15: "Several trips to a Fifth Avenue neurologist and two expensive, uncomfortable medical tests **had failed to produce a diagnosis**." **Failed to produce a diagnosis** means that

   a. the author did not pass his medical tests.

   b. the tests did not relieve his pain.

   c. the tests did not uncover his physical problem.

4. In lines 15–17, the neurologist suggested that the author see a bone doctor. In the next paragraph, what is a synonym for **bone doctor**?

   _____

5. Read lines 18–20: "During the hours spent waiting **in vain** to see an orthopedist, I decided to try acupuncture." **In vain** means

   a. uselessly.

   b. carefully.

   c. quietly.

6. In lines 30–31, the author writes, "A woman dancer was also getting a treatment." What does **treatment** mean?

   _____

7. In line 38, what are **Park Avenue** and **Mott Street**?

   a. similar places

   b. different places

   c. medical places

8. Read lines 39–40. "**In all** there are an estimated 10,000 acupuncturists in the country." What does **in all** mean?

   a. in total

   b. in fact

   c. in New York

9. Read lines 41–44: "Nowadays, a lot of M.D.s have learned acupuncture techniques; so have a number of dentists. Reason? Patient demand. Few, though, can adequately explain how acupuncture works."

   a. What does **nowadays** refer to?
      1. only at the present time
      2. from some time in the past up to the present
      3. during the time that the author's story takes place

   b. What are **M.D.s**?
      1. doctors
      2. dentists
      3. acupuncturists

   c. In line 43, who does **few** refer to?
      1. only patients
      2. only M.D.s
      3. dentists and M.D.s
      4. only dentists

10. Read lines 46 and 47: "A life force called *qi* (pronounced CHEE) circulates through the body."

    a. What is **qi**?

    _____

    b. How do you know?

    _____

11. Read lines 57–59: "Jack Tymann, 51, president and general manager of Westinghouse Electronic Systems Co., is typical." This sentence means that Jack Tymann is

    a. a common man.

    b. a common example.

    c. a common acupuncturist.

12. Read lines 60–61: "His doctor suggested disc surgery, but he decided to try acupuncture **instead**."

    a. Jack Tymann had
       1. surgery, but not acupuncture.
       2. surgery and acupuncture.
       3. acupuncture, but not surgery.

    b. Complete the following sentence correctly.

       Jack and Helen wanted to go to the beach, but it was raining. They decided to
       1. go to the movies instead.
       2. go for a walk instead.
       3. go for a swim instead.

13. Read lines 69–71: "Harwood Beville, 51, executive vice president of the Rouse Co., started acupuncture nine years ago, for treatment of 'what I'll call tennis shoulder.'" How old was Harwood Beville when he started acupuncture?

    a. 51

    b. 42

    c. 60

14. Read lines 78–80: "Acupuncture is used to treat a variety of **ailments**—anxiety, depression, back pain, smoking, high blood pressure, stress, arthritis; the list goes on." What are **ailments**?

    a. treatments

    b. problems

    c. illnesses

• C. Word Forms

Part 1

In English, verbs can change to nouns in several ways. Some verbs become nouns by adding the suffix *-ion* or *-tion*, for example, *prevent* (v.), *prevention* (n.).

Complete each sentence with the correct form of the words on the left. **Use the correct tense of the verbs, in either the affirmative or the negative form. Use the singular or plural form of the nouns.**

explain (v.)
explanation (n.)

1. a. Yesterday, the teacher _____ how electricity is produced because she didn't have time.

   b. Tomorrow, when she gives her scientific _____, I will take notes.

recommend (v.)
recommendation (n.)

2. a. John _____ that I take advanced calculus this semester, but I didn't listen to him.

   b. I should have taken his advice because his _____ have always been sensible.

stimulate (v.)
stimulation (n.)

3. a. Babies need constant _____ in order to help their development.

   b. If adults _____ babies' interest in the world around them, they will become more alert.

conclude (v.)
conclusion (n.)

4. a. Copernicus, a well-known Polish astronomer, _____ that the Earth was round.

   b. He reached his revolutionary _____ in the sixteenth century.

decide (v.)
decision (n.)

5. a. I _____ yet where to apply to graduate school.

   b. I need to make some other important _____ first, such as whether to stay in this country or go back home.

Part 2

In English, adjectives usually become adverbs by adding the suffix *-ly*, for example, *immediate* (adj.), *immediately* (adv.).

Complete each sentence with the correct form of the words on the left.

extreme (adj.)
extremely (adv.)

1. a. Some people believe that the death penalty is an _____ form of punishment.
   b. Others believe that murder is an_____ serious crime, and that murderers deserve capital punishment.

strange (adj.)
strangely (adv.)

2. a. Barbara has been acting very_____ lately. I wonder if anything is wrong.
   b. Perhaps I should ask her about her_____ behavior.

involuntary (adj.)
involuntarily (adv.)

3. a. Sometimes people jump when they hear thunder. This is called an_____ reaction.
   b. Other people react _____ when they see something unexpectedly.

adequate (adj.)
adequately (adv.)

4. a. This essay is clearly not _____. It should be at least 300 words.
   b. You cannot express your point of view _____ in only 100 words.

usual (adj.)
usually (adv.)

5. a. Eve _____, but not always, takes her vacation in August.
   b. This is because her _____ vacation consists of relaxing on the beach and swimming in the ocean.

• D. Dictionary Skills

Choose the appropriate definition for each word. Then write the number and the synonym or meaning in the space provided. **Be sure to use the correct form of the verbs and nouns.**

1. **conclude** *v*
   1 come or bring to an end: *He ~d by saying that . . .*   **2** arrange; bring about: *to ~ a treaty with . . .*   **3** arrive at a belief or opinion: *The jury ~d from the evidence, that the accused man was not guilty.*

   The neurologist (___) _____ that perhaps I leaned on my left arm

   too much and suggested that I see a bone doctor.

2. **hustle** *v*
   1 push or shove roughly: *The police ~d the thief into their van.*   **2** hurry; rush: *I don't want to ~ you into a decision.*   **3** (*informal*) sell or obtain something by energetic (and sometimes illegal) activity.

   Dr. Gong (___) _____ me into a room, had me lie down on a cot,

   and went to work.

3. **fail** *v*
   1 be unsuccessful: *All our plans ~ed.*   **2** grade (a student) as failing in a course, an examination, etc: *Students not taking the final exam will be ~ed.*   **3** be not enough; come to an end while still needed or expected: *The crops ~ed because of drought.*   **4** omit; neglect: *He never ~s to write* (= always writes) *to his mother every week.*

   Millions of Americans go to acupuncturists, usually because conven-

   tional medicine (___) _____. It does not cure their ills.

4. **dramatic** *adj*
   1 of drama: *~ performance.*   **2** sudden or exciting: *~ changes in the international situation.*   **3** (of a person, his speech, behavior) showing feelings or character in a lively way.

   After five treatments from Dr. Gong, there has been (___) _____

   improvement in my arm.

• E. Information Organization

Read the article a second time. Underline what you think are the main ideas. Then scan the article and complete the following outline, using the sentences that you have underlined to help you. You will use this outline later to answer specific questions about the article.

I. The Author's Thoughts About His First Acupuncture Experience

    A. How the treatment felt

        1.

        2.

    B. Why he had come to Dr. Gong's office

        1.

        2.

II. A Description of Today's Acupuncturists

    A.

    B.

    C.

III. A Description of Acupuncture

    A.

    B. A life force called *qi* (pronounced CHEE) circulates through the body

    C.

    D.

    E. Acupuncture is at least 2,200 years old, but nobody really knows how it works

IV. Who Gets Acupuncture Treatments

    A. number of people:

       usual reason:

    B. examples of people who have acupuncture treatments:

        1.

        2.

V. Uses of Acupuncture

    A.

    B.

VI. Effectiveness of Acupuncture

    A.

• F. Information Organization Quiz and Summary

Read each question carefully. Use your notes to answer the questions. Do not refer back to the text. Write your answers in the space provided under each question. When you are finished, write a brief summary of the article.

1. Why did the author decide to go to an acupuncturist?

    _____

    _____

    _____

2. What is acupuncture? How does it work?

    _____

    _____

    _____

3. a. Why did Jack Tymann go to an acupuncturist? What was the result of his treatments?

    _____

    _____

    _____

    b. Why did Harwood Beville go to an acupuncturist? What was the result of his treatments?

    _____

    _____

    _____

4. What is acupuncture used to treat?

    _____

    _____

    _____

5. How long do acupuncture treatments usually take?

    _____

    _____

    _____

Summary

_____

_____

_____

_____

• G. Critical Thinking Strategies

Read each question carefully. Write your response in the space provided. Remember that there is no one correct answer. Your response depends on what **you** think.

1. In the first paragraph of this passage, the author describes his acupuncture treatment. He writes, "Other needles were slipped into my left wrist and, **strangely**, my **right** arm, and then into both my closed eyelids." Why did he think this was strange?

_____

_____

_____

_____

2. In lines 12–17, the author talks about his experiences with a "Fifth Avenue neurologist." What do you think the author believed about Fifth Avenue doctors before he had acupuncture treatments?

_____

_____

_____

_____

3. In the third paragraph, the author describes his experience with the Fifth Avenue neurologist. In the fourth paragraph, he recounts his trip to Dr. Gong's office. The author gives different impressions about the two doctors and their environments. What are they?

_____

_____

_____

_____

4. According to this article, Harwood Beville went to an acupuncturist because other doctors could not help him and because "acupuncture had worked for his wife." How do you think Mrs. Beville's experience affected Mr. Beville?

_____

_____

_____

_____

5. Read the last two sentences of this article. What is the tone of these statements? In other words, what is the author's opinion about Dr. Gong?

_____

_____

_____

• H. Follow-up Discussion and Activities

1. *Jigsaw Reading:* You are going to read more information about acupuncture: what it is, how it works, and what it treats.

   a. First, all students read the paragraph titled *Acupuncture.* Discuss it in class to make sure everyone understands it.

   b. Second, work in a group of three or four students. Each group will read different information about acupuncture. Group A will read about what acupuncture is; Group B will read about how acupuncture works; Group C will read about what acupuncture treats. If your class is large, then you may have more than one Group A, B, or C; just make sure that at least one group reads about each segment on acupuncture. After reading the paragraph, discuss it to make sure everyone in the group understands about their particular segment.

   c. Third, set up different groups so that each group has a student or students who have read each paragraph. In these new groups, tell each other what you have read about acupuncture. In the spaces under your paragraph, take notes about the information the other students give you. Do not look back at your readings. Ask each other questions to make sure that all the students in your group understand all the information about acupuncture.

   d. Finally, work together to answer the questions on page 91. When your group is finished, compare your answers with the other groups' answers.

All Students Read: *Acupuncture*

Acupuncture is a scientific and complete system based on exact laws and principles. It has been used in China for centuries. In fact, classical Chinese acupuncture is one of the oldest forms of medicine known to mankind.

Group A Only: *What Is Acupuncture?*

Acupuncture is a system of medicine used to restore and maintain health, as well as prevent illness. It originated in China over 5,000 years ago and is based on the belief that any illness or symptom is associated with an imbalance in the body's vital life energy. Traditional acupuncture works to restore the natural flow of this energy throughout the body, relieving the underlying cause of the illness and the accompanying symptoms.

Group B's Information:

_____

_____

_____

_____

_____

_____

Group C's Information:

_____

_____

_____

_____

_____

_____

Group B Only: *How Does Acupuncture Work?*

The vital energy, known as "Ch'i" energy, travels in twelve pathways called "meridians." Each meridian corresponds to a vital organ, such as kidneys, liver, heart, stomach, lungs, etc. Each has a pulse that informs the acupuncturist of the condition of the energy within that meridian. When the acupuncturist inserts very fine needles into points that lie along these meridians, energy is summoned to the places that need it and dispersed from the areas where it is congested. In this way the natural flow of energy along the pathways is restored and healthy patterns reestablished over time.

Group A's Information:

_____

_____

_____

_____

_____

_____

_____

_____

Group C's Information:

_____

_____

_____

_____

_____

_____

_____

_____

Group C Only: *What Does Acupuncture Treat?*

Acupuncture treats the whole person—the body, the mind, and the spirit—therefore, it can be helpful in the treatment of all conditions. In addition to its widespread use in the relief of pain, acupuncture has been used to treat a wide variety of illnesses both as a primary modality and as an adjunct to traditional western medicine. Acupuncture is useful in treating chronic conditions, e.g., headaches, chronic fatigue, anxiety, and insomnia. It increases energy levels, assists the immune system, and contributes to a person's general well-being.

Group A's Information:

_____
_____
_____
_____
_____
_____
_____
_____

Group B's Information:

_____
_____
_____
_____
_____
_____
_____

Acupuncture Questions

1. What is acupuncture?

_____

_____

2. When did it originate?

_____

_____

3. What belief is acupuncture based on?

_____

_____

4. What is "Ch'i" energy?

_____

_____

5. What is a meridian?

_____

_____

6. How is acupuncture done?

_____

_____

7. How does acupuncture help the patient?

_____

_____

_____

8. How does acupuncture treat the whole person?

_____

_____

9. What illnesses does acupuncture help?

_____

_____

10. What other problems does acupuncture treat?

_____

_____

2. Many people today are using traditional forms of medicine in place of modern treatments. What do you think are some reasons for this change? Write a composition to explain your answer.

3. a. In a group, make a list of common illnesses. Next to each illness, write the traditional forms of medicine that you know are used to treat these illnesses, both in your country and in other countries. Then write the modern treatments for these illnesses. Compare the two types of treatment for each illness you have chosen. For instance, which treatment is usually less expensive? Which usually takes less time to see positive results? Which seems to be more effective? Which is less extreme, i.e., involves taking medicine or getting therapy, as opposed to having surgery?

   b. For each illness, discuss which type of treatment you would prefer if you had that illness. Explain your reasons to your classmates.

   c. As a class, list on the blackboard all the illnesses that you discussed and the traditional and modern treatments for each. Then take a poll to see how many students prefer the traditional treatments and how many students prefer the modern treatments for these ailments.

4. Select a traditional form of medicine that has been used in your country for a long time. Describe its uses and its effectiveness. Discuss your personal experience with this traditional form, or the experience of someone you know. Tell whether you would recommend this form of medicine to others, and why.

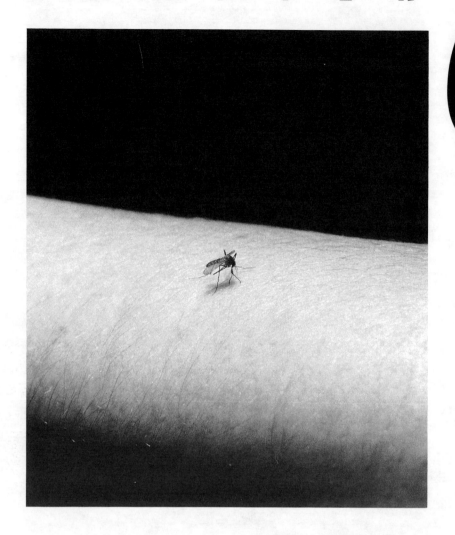

Mosquito With a Mission

by John F. Lauerman
Health

• Prereading Preparation

1. Where do you find mosquitoes? What kind of climate do they live in?
2. What is **malaria**? How can you get it? Is it fatal? Is it common today?
3. What diseases do you know of that were fatal in the past but that are either preventable or curable today? Describe them.

1   In film and literature, malaria, the mosquito-borne dis-
2 ease, has an exotic sound. It calls to mind images of Brit-
3 ish colonial coffee plantations in Africa or courageous
4 explorers sailing down the Amazon, taking quinine pills
5 and sleeping at night under mosquito nets. In reality, the
6 disease—which can cause acute fever and chills, headache,
7 muscle ache, fatigue, and, sometimes, death—has created
8 a public-health crisis in the tropical and subtropical re-
9 gions of the globe where it is gaining in force each year.
10   There were 1,102 cases of malaria in the United States
11 in 1989. Globally, the statistics are much more serious.
12 More than 100 million people in areas like Egypt, southern
13 Africa, parts of Southeast Asia, India, Central America,
14 Papua New Guinea and Mexico suffer from malaria each
15 year, and nearly two million of them die. In Africa, one
16 quarter of all children between the ages of one and four
17 dies from it. In Sri Lanka, where international spraying and
18 drug distribution programs once reduced the number of
19 annual cases to 17, there are now an estimated three quar-
20 ters of a million cases of malaria per year.
21   Malaria is neither a virus like polio nor a bacterium like
22 tuberculosis. Rather, it's a parasite[1] that invades red blood

---

[1]parasite: an organism that grows and feeds on or in a different organism but contributes nothing to the survival of that organism.

23 cells and has a three-stage life cycle. Infection starts out
24 with a mosquito bite that releases a few of the parasites
25 into the human bloodstream. The invaders travel to the
26 liver where the body's cells hide them from the immune
27 system, allowing them to multiply. Soon afterwards, the
28 parasites burst out of the liver, and attack red blood cells.
29 These, too, eventually burst and release still more para-
30 sites, triggering malaria's symptoms.
31   In the 1950s, malaria was believed to be on the verge of
32 eradication. The introduction of insecticides such as DDT
33 seemed to signal the end of the malaria-carrying mosquito
34 in certain countries. Even if you had contracted malaria,
35 you could have been cured with chloroquine, a synthetic
36 quinine-like drug.
37   Forty years later, malaria is making a comeback. The
38 parasite has developed a resistance to familiar pesticides
39 like DDT and to chloroquine. As a precaution, travelers
40 continue to take chloroquine or other drugs prior to, dur-
41 ing and after leaving a malarious area. In areas where ma-
42 laria is drug-resistant, new medications are needed and
43 many researchers say a vaccine is a must. Developing an
44 effective one could save hundreds of thousands of lives.
45   Currently, researchers are investigating three possible
46 plans of attack for a vaccine. One would kill the parasites,
47 before they enter the liver cells and while they're in them.
48 Another would attack the parasite in its second stage, de-
49 stroying infected red blood cells. The third would create
50 antibodies that would be ingested by a biting mosquito and
51 stop the mature parasites from developing. However, no
52 one has yet found the formula for an effective inoculation.
53   Most vaccines, like those for smallpox or polio, consist
54 of dead or modified forms of the same dangerous bugs that
55 cause the disease. The vaccine helps the immune system
56 recognize and attack the invader. However, previous re-
57 search has shown that standard types of vaccines are inef-
58 fective against malaria because the infected mosquitoes
59 don't carry enough of the parasite to create a useful vaccine.
60   One of the more interesting approaches to the problem
61 is that of Manuel Patarroyo, M.D., founder and director of
62 the Institute of Immunology in Bogota, Colombia. In 1986
63 he created a synthetic vaccine, hoping that the body's own
64 immune cells would kill the parasite.
65   Perhaps because a malaria vaccine seems far in the fu-
66 ture, many experts are suggesting that attention should

67 continue to be focused on areas like prevention, control
68 and treatment. One new strategy for controlling transmis-
69 sion is pesticide-treated bed nets, which protect sleeping
70 people from mosquitoes and kill any bugs that happen to
71 land on the net.
72   Some researchers are exploring folklore treatments in
73 the hopes of developing stronger drugs. Derivatives of
74 qing-hao, a weed used in traditional Chinese medicine to
75 treat fever, are being studied by scientists.
76   While these approaches are promising, none have
77 proven tough enough to stop malaria. Until researchers
78 find the parasite's Achilles heel, the disease will continue
79 to infect millions.

• A. Fact-Finding Exercise

Read the passage once. Then read the following statements. Scan the article quickly to find out if each statement is true (T) or false (F). If a statement is false, change it so that it is true.

_____ T _____ F   1. Malaria is a disease that is increasing each year.

_____ T _____ F   2. One hundred million people die of malaria each year.

_____ T _____ F   3. A person can get malaria from a mosquito bite.

_____ T _____ F   4. In the 1950s, malaria was curable.

_____ T _____ F   5. Researchers have found a vaccine for malaria.

_____ T _____ F   6. Specially treated bed nets can cure malaria.

• B. Reading Analysis

Read each question carefully. Circle the number or letter of the correct answer, or write your answer in the space provided.

1. Read the first paragraph. The author contrasts the reality of malaria with its image in film and literature. What does he think about film and literature?

   a. They show the truth about malaria.
   b. They show a false image of malaria.

2. Read lines 1–5.

   a. In the first sentence, **sound** means
      1. noise.
      2. implication.
      3. voice.

   b. **It calls to mind** means
      1. malaria gives us a mental picture.
      2. malaria is the name of the disease.
      3. malaria tells us something.

3. Read lines 12–13. Why does **southern** Africa begin with a lower-case *s* while **Southeast** Asia begins with an upper case *s*?

   _____

4. In line 15, **nearly** means
   a. almost.
   b. more than.
   c. at least.

5. In lines 15–16, **one quarter** is
   a. an age.
   b. an amount
   c. a number

6. In line 17, what is **it**?

   _____

7. Read lines 22 and 23.

   a. What is a parasite?

   _____

   b. How do you know?

   _____

    c. This type of information is called a
       1. preface.
       2. footnote.
       3. direction.

8. Read lines 22–27. What are **the invaders**?
   a. the bloodstream
   b. the mosquitos
   c. the parasites

9. Read lines 31 and 32. **On the verge of eradication** means that malaria
   a. was very strong.
   b. was disappearing.
   c. was increasing

10. Read lines 34–36. This information
   a. is no longer true.
   b. is still true today.

11. Read line 37: "Malaria is making a comeback." This means that malaria
   a. is changing its symptoms.
   b. is showing up in other countries.
   c. is returning.

12. Read lines 37–39: "The parasite has developed a resistance to familiar pesticides like DDT and to chloroquine." This sentence means that
   a. DDT and chloroquine are still useful against malaria.
   b. DDT and chloroquine are not useful against malaria anymore.

13. Read lines 41–43. The expression **a must** means
   a. an idea.
   b. a necessity.
   c. a difficulty.

14. Read lines 45–49. What do **one** and **another** refer to?

_____

15. Read lines 72–75.

   a. What is **qing-hao**?

_____

   b. How do you know?

_____

• C. Word Forms

Part 1

In English, the verb and noun forms of some words are the same, for example, *experience* (v.), *experience* (n.).

Complete each sentence with the correct form of the words on the left. **Use the correct tense of the verbs, in either the affirmative or the negative form. Use the singular or plural form of the nouns. In addition, indicate whether you are using the verb form or the noun form of the word.**

cure

1. a. Penicillin _____ influenza because
   (v., n.)
   the flu is caused by a virus, not a bacterium.

   b. Right now, there are many diseases that
   scientists haven't found an effective
   _____ for yet.
   (v., n.)

focus

2. a. Emily carefully _____ the camera
   (v., n.)
   on her friend, then took a photograph.

   b. The _____ of her camera was very
   (v., n.)
   sharp, and the picture was very clear.

gain

3. a. Tom was very upset by his sudden
   _____ in weight—15 pounds.
   (v., n.)

   b. He _____ the weight while he was
   (v., n.)
   on vacation; he got heavier while he was home.

release

4. a. Premier Pictures _____ a new film next
   (v., n.)
   season. I've heard that it's a murder mystery.

   b. Premier hasn't put out any new _____
   (v., n.)
   in the last six months, which is surprising.

signal

5. a. The drivers are waiting for the race to
   start, but the flagman _____ yet.
   (v., n.)

   b. Once the flagman gives the appropriate
   _____ for the race to begin, the drivers
   (v., n.)
   will accelerate onto the track.

Part 2

In English, some adjectives become nouns by adding the suffix *-ity*, for example, *public* (adj.), *publicity* (n.).

Complete each sentence with the correct form of the words on the left. **Use the singular or plural form of the nouns.**

impossible (adj.)
impossibility (n.)

1. a. Jesse said that it is absolutely _____ for him to take a vacation this year.
   b. However, his wife doesn't seem to think it's such a complete _____, and she is making plans anyway.

real (adj.)
reality (n.)

2. a. Harriet would like to quit her job and go back to school full time, but the _____ of the situation is that she has to continue working.
   b. If she stopped working, she would have a _____ problem in paying her bills.

fatal (adj.)
fatality (n.)

3. a. Jim heard about a _____ accident at the airport over the radio.
   b. Apparently, an airplane crashed on takeoff, resulting in many injuries but no _____.

individual (adj.)
individuality (n.)

4. a. Anna wants to go to a small college because she feels she will receive more personal, _____ attention.
   b. Furthermore, Anna believes that small colleges have a special _____ of their own.

able (adj.)
ability (n.)

5. a. If Bob has a problem with his car, he is usually quite _____ to fix it himself.
   b. He developed this mechanical _____ by working on his father's car when he was younger.

• D. Dictionary Skills

Choose the appropriate definition for each word. Then write the number and the synonym or meaning in the space provided. **Be sure to use the correct form of the verbs and nouns.**

1. **force** *n*

1 strength; power of body or mind: *the ~ of a blow/an explosion/argument. The enemy attacked in (great) ~.* **2** person or thing that makes great changes; strong influence: *the ~es of nature,* e.g. storms, earthquakes. **3** organized body of armed or disciplined men and women: *the armed ~s of a country.* **4** (intensity of, measurement of) pressure or influence: *the ~ of gravity.*

Malaria is gaining in (____)_____ in the subtropical regions of the globe.

2. **gain** *v*

1 obtain (something wanted or needed): *~ experience; ~ an advantage over a competitor.* **2** increase in weight, speed, etc: *The baby ~ed five pounds.* **3** (of a watch or clock) run fast, ahead of the correct time: *The clock ~s three minutes a day.*

Malaria (____)_____ in force each year in the subtropical regions of the globe.

3. **release** *v*

1 allow to go; set free: *~ one's grip/a man from prison.* **2** relieve, as from a promise or obligation. **3** make available for publication, exhibition, or sale: *recently ~ed film/news.* **4** give up or surrender (a right, debt, property) to another.

A mosquito bite (____)_____ a few of the malaria parasites into the human bloodstream.

4. **burst** *v*

1 (of a bomb, shell, etc) (cause to) fly or break violently apart from within; explode. **2** (of river banks, a dam) (cause to) break outwards; (of a bubble) break; (of leaf and flower buds) open out. **3** be full to overflowing; be able to contain with difficulty: *They were ~ing with happiness/impatience.* **4** make a way or entry suddenly or by force: *He ~ into the room. The sun ~ through the clouds.*

The parasites multiply in the liver. Soon afterwards, the parasites (____)_____ out of the liver and attack red blood cells.

• E. Information Organization

Read the article a second time. Underline what you think are the main ideas. Then scan the article and fill in the following flowchart, using the sentences that you have underlined to help you. You will use this flowchart later to answer specific questions about the article.

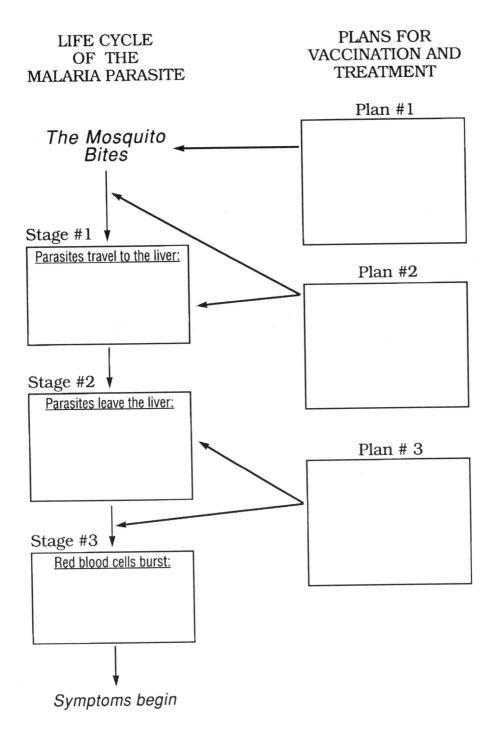

LIFE CYCLE
OF THE
MALARIA PARASITE

PLANS FOR
VACCINATION AND
TREATMENT

The Mosquito Bites

Plan #1

Stage #1

Parasites travel to the liver:

Plan #2

Stage #2

Parasites leave the liver:

Plan # 3

Stage #3

Red blood cells burst:

Symptoms begin

• F. Information Organization Quiz and Summary

Read each question carefully. Use your flowchart to answer the questions. Do not refer back to the text. Write your answers in the space provided under each question. When you are finished, write a brief summary of the article.

1. How do people get malaria?

   _____

   _____

2. Describe the life cycle of the malaria parasite.

   _____

   _____

   _____

3. Describe the vaccination and treatment plans for malaria.

   _____

   _____

   _____

4. What stage in the parasite's life cycle do these plans affect?

   _____

   _____

   _____

Summary

_____

_____

_____

_____

_____

• G. Critical Thinking Strategies

Read each question carefully. Write your response in the space provided. Remember that there is no one correct answer. Your response depends on what **you** think.

1. The article states that "in Sri Lanka, where international spraying and drug distribution programs once reduced the number of annual cases to 17, there are now an estimated three quarters of a million [750,000] cases of malaria per year." What is implied by this information? In other words, what do you think happened in Sri Lanka because there were so few cases of malaria? Why do you think the number of cases of malaria has risen so dramatically?

_____

_____

_____

_____

2. At the end of the article, the author tells how "researchers are exploring folklore treatments in the hopes of developing stronger drugs. Derivatives of qing-hao, a weed used in traditional Chinese medicine to treat fever, are being studied by scientists." What do you think researchers believe about folklore treatments and traditional medicine?

_____

_____

_____

_____

3. Achilles was a hero in Greek mythology. When Achilles was born, his mother tried to make him strong by submerging him in the magical River Styx. Unfortunately, she held him by his heel, which did not get wet. Achilles' heel was his only weak spot. In the end, Achilles was killed by an arrow that was shot into his heel. Today, the expression "Achilles heel" means a weak spot. Why do you think the author referred to an Achilles heel in the last paragraph when speaking about the malaria parasite?

_____

_____

_____

_____

4. This article discusses Dr. Manuel Patarroyo's approach to the problem of malaria. Why do you think his idea of a synthetic vaccine is interesting? How do you think a synthetic vaccine is different from other common vaccines, such as those for smallpox or polio?

_____

_____

_____

_____

• H. Follow-up Discussion and Activities

1. a. Certain illnesses are more common in some countries than others. Work alone or with a classmate from your country. Make a list of illnesses that are more common in your country than in other countries. Describe these diseases, and explain why you think they occur more frequently.

   b. Combine the class list of diseases on the blackboard, along with their descriptions. Indicate whether the diseases are contagious and/or fatal.

2. a. Work in a small group. You are a panel of international medical experts working for the World Health Organization. Your task is to focus on one disease that the WHO will focus on and try to eliminate. In your group, decide which disease is the most important one to cure. Be sure that you can support your opinion.

   b. Get back into one group with the class. Discuss the disease that your group has chosen to eliminate. As a single group, decide which disease your united panel will focus on.

• Library Resource Mastery

The reference area of the library includes such materials as dictionaries, atlases, almanacs, and encyclopedias. An encyclopedia gives more detailed information than an almanac. Encyclopedias are updated periodically, but because they are expensive, the encyclopedias in a library may be several years old. However, an almanac is updated every year. On the other hand, the information it contains is very brief. Consequently, these two reference sources work well together: an encyclopedia provides detailed background information, and an almanac gives up-to-date, concise information.

• Library Assignment

1. a. Go to the reference section of the library. Ask the librarian where the encyclopedia and the almanac are located.

    b. Use the encyclopedia to get background information on one or two diseases that you are interested in learning more about. Refer to the following Disease Chart. Fill in the appropriate spaces for the information that you have collected.

    c. Refer next to the almanac. Look up the diseases in the Disease Chart. Find the latest medical discoveries that have helped people treat and/or cure these diseases.

    d. Report your findings to the class. Compare the information you obtained on each disease.

DISEASE	Countries/areas where it is widespread	How it is caused	Number of cases reported annually	Cure and/or treatment

Unit II Review

• I. Vocabulary Categorization

The words in the vocabulary list below have been taken from the three readings in this unit. Read through the list, and place the words into the three categories indicated. Write in the appropriate heading for the category that has been left blank. Some words may fit into more than one category.

ailment	expert	recommendation
arthritis	explanation	region
attitude	fatality	responsibility
conclusion	fault	strategy
cure	importance	suggestion
decade	individual	surgery
decision	medicine	symptom
depression	myth	tradition
disease	pain	treatment
education	prevention	

Discussion/Advice   **Custom/Culture**   _____

• J. Crossword Puzzle

Across

1. Traditional
4. The opposite of **down**
6. He, _____, it
10. The opposite of **no**
13. Apathetic; uncaring
14. Not do something you should do
16. Illness; disease
18. The way an acupuncturist handles an illness is the manner of _____.
19. However
23. The opposite of **off**
26. He, she, ____
27. Useless; without result
28. An organism that feeds on another organism
30. The opposite of **yes**
31. _____ is the crime of deliberately setting a fire.
32. Sick; not well
35. State of mind; way of thinking about something
36. Doctors perform _____ when they do an operation.

Down

2. A _____ is a type of inoculation.
3. The opposite of **out**
5. Stop from happening
7. Elimination
8. The past of **have**
9. I _____ speak English well.
11. Punishment; fine
12. A safety measure
15. Mistake
17. Both women and _____ go to acupuncturists.
20. The body's immune system creates _____ to protect it against disease.
21. The opposite of **on**
22. When a doctor gives a _____, she is describing your illness.
24. Licensed
25. Discourage; try to stop
28. The past of **pay**
29. Mary was tired, _____ she went to bed.
33. The opposite of **win**
34. They _____ getting acupuncture treatments.
35. Every; each

• K. Unit II Discussion

1. Even though we live in a modern world, we are still faced with such basic dangers and health threats as fire, illness and pain, and insect-borne diseases. Discuss what you think is the biggest threat to you, your family, or your country. What, if anything, are people doing about it? Do you think they are doing enough? What else can people do?

2. In Chapter 5, the author turned to acupuncture, a traditional treatment for pain, after modern medical treatments did not work. In Chapter 6, the author discusses treating malaria with traditional medicines such as *qing-hao*. Many people use the aloe plant as a traditional treatment for minor burns. Why do you think there is a trend toward using traditional medical treatments?

Government and Education

C·H·A·P·T·E·R 7

The Federal System of Government

by Patricia C. Acheson

from *Our Federal Government: How It Works*

• Prereading Preparation

1. How did the United States become an independent country?
2. a. Who were the first Europeans in the United States?

   b. Why did they come to the United States?
3. a. What kind of government does the United States have?

   b. What do you know about this type of government?
4. What is a **constitution**? Why do governments have constitutions? What is their usual purpose?
5. Take a survey in your class. On the blackboard, write the name of the country each student is from. Then, write the type of government each country has. Which countries have the same type of government? Which countries have the same type of government as the United States?

1   What is the government of the United States exactly?
2 How and when did it come to be? Who were the people
3 who agreed to accept our government and why did they
4 want to accept it?
5   The answers to these questions lie in the events that
6 took place between 1775 and 1787. In 1775 the war against
7 British domination began. At that point there was no cen-
8 tral American government established by law. There was
9 only the Continental Congress made up of men who be-
10 lieved in independence and who were willing to fight for
11 their cause. It was that Congress that declared the colonies
12 independent of Great Britain in July, 1776, and it was only
13 after that decision that the evolution of our present form of
14 government began. The initial step was to establish legal
15 governments in the states to replace colonial rule. The

16 states established republics; each of the thirteen new states
17 had elected governors and representative assemblies.
18   The Continental Congress was without legal founda-
19 tion, and it was necessary to establish some form of over-
20 all government agreed to by the people and speaking for
21 all the states. However, the Americans of this period reluc-
22 tantly accepted this necessity, as the majority believed
23 that they could guarantee their freedom only if each state
24 remained almost entirely independent of the others.
25   Therefore, the first government of the United States
26 under the Articles of Confederation adopted in 1781 was
27 very restricted in its authority. It consisted of a Congress
28 made up of representatives from the states. There was no
29 president with certain specific powers, only a chairman
30 whose job it was to preside and to keep order. The Con-
31 gress had very little power to do anything. Congress could
32 not pass tax laws; it did not have the sole authority to coin
33 money for use by the states, nor could it regulate trade
34 between the states. Because it had no money of its own,
35 the Congress could not pay any of its debts, it could not
36 borrow money, and it could not pay an army or a navy.
37   Within four years after the end of the war in 1783, it
38 became obvious that the system of government under the
39 Articles of Confederation was not working out. The discon-
40 tent and the fact that the new nation was extraordinarily
41 weak without an adequate army or navy made thoughtful
42 people realize that a better government must be worked
43 out if the United States of America was to be a strong and
44 rich nation. In Philadelphia in 1787 a convention, or meet-
45 ing, was held in order to reshape the government. It was
46 there that our present system of government was born,
47 and the Constitution of the United States was written. The
48 people of the United States are still governed today by the
49 framework drawn up in that document over two hundred
50 years ago.

51 **The Constitution**
52   The foreword to the Constitution stated the democratic
53 principles to be followed by the United States government.
54 The government must insure freedom for the citizens of
55 the United States for all times.
56   To create such a government was not an easy thing to
57 do. Remember that in 1787 the men at the convention in
58 Philadelphia were pioneers in the setting up of a demo-

59 cratic republican government. They really only knew what
60 they did not want. They did not want a king, and they did
61 not want too strong a central government because they
62 were afraid of losing their own freedoms. They certainly
63 wanted to keep the states as they were. To erase them
64 would have been impossible. Each colony had its own in-
65 dividuality and pride. There could be no question of mak-
66 ing just one government and forgetting the individual
67 states. On the other hand, the men in Philadelphia knew
68 that the first government set up under the Articles of Con-
69 federation had had too little power to carry out its busi-
70 ness, and no one had been satisfied.
71   Here was a dilemma. On the one hand, it seemed that a
72 strong central government was very undesirable because it
73 might endanger the people's liberties. On the other hand, a
74 weak central government had proven inadequate. The solu-
75 tion these men found is called the "checks and balance" sys-
76 tem, and it is the heart and soul of the Constitution.

77 The Checks and Balance System

78   The writers of the Constitution wanted to make sure
79 that the people's rights would always be safe and that the
80 central or federal government would never become too
81 powerful. A government ought to have three major pow-
82 ers: to make laws, to carry out those laws, and to provide
83 justice under law for the best interests of the people.
84 Should these three functions be in the hands of one person
85 or one group, there would be great danger that that person
86 or group could use the power for personal profit rather
87 than for the people. To guard against this possibility, the
88 Constitution provided for three major branches of govern-
89 ment: the legislature, or congress, to make laws; the execu-
90 tive to carry out the laws; and the judiciary to watch over
91 the rights of the people as described in the Constitution.
92   The powers of these three branches of the government
93 are described carefully in the Constitution. To make sure
94 that the government should never take more power than it
95 was granted in the Constitution, it was carefully stated that
96 any power not given to the government should forever be-
97 long to the states. Another reason for describing carefully
98 the powers of the three branches was to prevent any one
99 branch from becoming stronger than the others. Each job
100 in the running of the country was balanced between the
101 legislative, the executive and the judicial branches. Each

102 part of the government can only function in relation to the
103 others. This system not only balances power between the
104 three branches, but also provides a check on each branch
105 by the others. A good example of the check system can be
106 found in the manner in which laws become laws. The leg-
107 islature, or Congress, has the job of drafting laws for the
108 country. Once a bill[1] has been passed by the two houses,
109 the Senate and the House of Representatives, the Congress
110 must send a copy to the chief executive, the president of
111 the United States, for his approval. He then has several op-
112 tions as to what he may do. For instance, he may agree
113 with the bill and sign the copy, in which case the law goes
114 into effect. Or, if he should feel that it is not a good law, he
115 may veto it. Vetoing means that he refuses to sign. Should
116 he do that, the copy is returned to the house of Congress
117 in which it originated. If the Congress, sure that the pro-
118 posed law is a necessary one, passes it again by a two-
119 thirds majority, the bill becomes law regardless of the
120 president's veto. The people are represented in Congress,
121 and if they still favor the law, it is more democratic that
122 they should have it.
123   The checks system goes further. The judicial branch
124 has its say about the laws of the land. Once the Congress
125 and the president have agreed upon a law, it must be en-
126 forced all over the United States. If someone disagrees with
127 a federal law and challenges it by disobeying it, the case is
128 brought into the court system of the United States. If the
129 Supreme Court decides to hear the case, it has the duty of
130 examining the law and determining if it is constitutional,
131 or in other words, whether the law is in keeping with the
132 rights of the people as outlined in the Constitution.
133   This system of balanced power and of checks between
134 the branches of the government means that at all times the
135 people's rights and interests are being carefully guarded. It
136 must be stressed, however, that as Thomas Jefferson[2] said,
137 "Eternal vigilance is the price of liberty," and if the people
138 of the United States, their elected representatives, and
139 their judges are not constantly vigilant, no mere words on
140 paper are going to protect their freedom.

---

[1]A bill is the name given to a law before it is signed by the president.

[2]Thomas Jefferson was the principal writer of the Declaration of Independence and the third president of the United States.

• A. Fact-Finding Exercise

Read the passage once. Then read the following statements. Scan the article quickly to find out if each statement is true (T) or false (F). If a statement is false, change it so that it is true.

_____ T _____ F   1. The United States became independent in 1775.

_____ T _____ F   2. The first U.S. government did not have a president.

_____ T _____ F   3. The United States' present government began in 1787.

_____ T _____ F   4. The U.S. Constitution described two branches of the government: the legislative and the judicial.

_____ T _____ F   5. The system of checks and balance prevents one branch of government from becoming too powerful.

_____ T _____ F   6. If the president disagrees with a new bill, it can never become a law.

• B. Reading Analysis

Read each question carefully. Circle the number or letter of the correct answer, or write your answer in the space provided.

1. Read lines 5–8. What does **at that point** mean?
   a. 1775
   b. 1787
   c. between 1775 and 1787

2. Read lines 8–14.
   a. What was the men's **cause**?

   _____

   b. In line 11, what does **that Congress** refer to?

   _____

3. Read lines 14–15.
   a. **Initial** means
      1. a letter of the alphabet.
      2. the first.
      3. the most difficult.

   b. **Rule** means
      1. law.
      2. state.
      3. colony.

   c. This sentence means that the people wanted to
      1. start new governments instead of the colonial government.
      2. establish the colonial government again.
      3. get rid of all forms of government.

4. Read lines 18–19: "The Continental Congress was without legal foundation." This sentence means that
   a. the Continental Congress broke the law.
   b. the Continental Congress did not make laws.
   c. the Continental Congress had no legal authority.

5. Read lines 21–27.

   a. In lines 21–22, **reluctantly** means
      1. recently.
      2. unanimously.
      3. unwillingly.

b. Complete the following sentence:

Gary wanted to find a job in New York because he thinks it is an exciting city. When he was unable to find a job there, he reluctantly
1. accepted a job in New Jersey.
2. continued looking for a job.

c. In line 22, **majority** means
1. some of the people.
2. more than half of the people.
3. all of the people.

d. In line 25, **therefore** means
1. furthermore.
2. in addition.
3. as a result.

6. Read lines 28–30. **Whose** refers to
   a. the president
   b. the chairman
   c. the Congress

7. Read lines 30–36. What types of control was the Congress not given?

_____

_____

_____

8. Read lines 37–44.

   a. In lines 39–40, **discontent** means
      1. discomfort.
      2. dissatisfaction.
      3. disagreement.

   b. Why were the people discontented?

   _____

9. Read lines 56–58. **Pioneers** are people who
   a. create new systems of government.
   b. set things up based on what they do not want.
   c. do something that no one has ever done before.

10. Read lines 70–75.

   a. What is a **dilemma**?
      1. It is a problem with two possible good solutions.
      2. It is a problem with two difficulties and one good solution.
      3. It is a problem with two possible solutions, neither of which is perfect.

   b. What follows **on the one hand** and **on the other hand**?
      1. the two possible solutions to the problem
      2. two good solutions to the problem
      3. two bad solutions to the problem

   c. What is **the heart and soul of the Constitution**?

   _____

11. Read lines 82–85. What are **hands**?
   a. law
   b. control
   c. body parts

12. Read lines 106–109.

   a. What is a **bill**?

   _____

   b. How do you know?

   _____

   c. This type of information is called a

   _____

13. Read lines 109–120

   a. What does **veto** mean?

   _____

   b. In line 117, **regardless of** means
      1. in addition to
      2. because of.
      3. in spite of.

   c. Complete the following sentence:
      Thomas wanted to go to the beach with his friends. He heard on the radio that it might rain in the afternoon. He decided to go to the beach regardless of
      1. the weather report.
      2. his friends.

14. Read lines 135–137.

    a. Who was Thomas Jefferson?

    _____

    b. Where did you find this information?

    _____

• C. Word Forms

Part 1

In English, verbs can change to nouns in several ways. Some verbs become nouns by adding the suffix -*ment*, for example, *equip* (v.), *equipment* (n.)
 Complete each sentence with the correct form of the words on the left. **Use the correct tense of the verbs, in either the affirmative or the negative form. Use the singular or plural form of the nouns.**

establish (v.)
establishment (n.)

1. a. Next year, the university _____ a new scholarship fund for foreign students.
    b. The permanent _____ of this type of scholarship fund will enable more students to study in this country.

agree (v.)
agreement (n.)

2. a. Tony _____ with us about going to the movies last night. In fact, we had an argument about it.
    b. We finally reached a mutual _____ after we found a movie that Tony really wanted to see.

replace (v.)
replacement (n.)

3. a. When my car broke down, I took it to the mechanic, who said that the carburetor needed _____.
    b. He not only _____ the carburetor, but he also tuned up the engine, and it cost me $800!

pay (v.)
payment (n.)

4. a. At registration, Phoebe _____ the full cost of her tuition at once.
    b. She arranged to cover her tuition in several _____ over four months.

enforce (v.)
enforcement (n.)

5. a. Rebecca is doing a study on law _____ for her master's thesis.
    b. She has discovered that some police precincts _____ the law as effectively as other precincts do.

Part 2

In English, some adjectives become nouns by deleting the final *-t* and adding *-ce*, for example, *competent* (adj.), *competence* (n.).

Complete each sentence with the correct form of the words on the left. **Use the singular form of the nouns.**

reluctant (adj.)

reluctance (n.)

1. a. Charles felt quite _____ about driving alone from New York to Chicago to attend a conference. We all understood his unwillingness to travel so far by himself.

   b. Because of his _____ to drive alone, he decided to take the train instead.

vigilant (adj.)

vigilance (n.)

2. a. It has rained so little in California for the last six years that forest rangers need to be especially _____ in watching for forest fires.

   b. Unfortunately, in spite of their around-the-clock _____, fires have started and gotten out of control, causing the loss of thousands of acres of forest.

resistant (adj.)

resistance (n.)

3. a. My grandparents are quite _____ to any kind of change.

   b. Sometimes their _____ is humorous. For example, they refuse to buy a new car, even though theirs is 30 years old and always breaks down when they drive into town. When the phone rings on Saturday morning, we always know who it is.

distant (adj.)

distance (n.)

4. a. Julie called her parents long _____ last night.

   b. Unfortunately, the connection was very poor; their voices sounded so _____ that Julie hung up and tried the call again.

• D. Dictionary Skills

Read the dictionary entry for each word. Indicate the number of the definition and write the synonym or meaning in the space provided. Remember that you may need to change the wording of the definition in order to have a grammatically correct sentence.

1. **cause** *n*

1 **a** a reason for an action or condition: MOTIVE **b** something that brings about an effect or a result **c** a person or thing that is the occasion of an action or state; *esp*: an agent that brings something about **2 a** a ground of legal action **b** CASE **3** a matter or question to be decided **4** a principle or movement militantly defended or supported

The Continental Congress was made up of men who believed in independence and who believed very strongly in the (____)_____that they supported.

2. **assembly** *n*
   pl **-blies**

1 a company of persons gathered for deliberation and legislation, worship, or entertainment **2** a legislative body; *specif*: the lower house of a legislature **3** ASSEMBLAGE 1, 2 **4** a signal for troops to assemble or fall in **5** the fitting together of manufactured parts into a complete machine, structure, or unit of a machine **b** a collection of parts so assembled

The thirteen new states had elected governors and representative (____)_____.

3. **erase** *vb*
   erased; eras-ing

1 **a** to rub or scrape out (as written, painted, or engraved letters) **b** to remove (recorded matter) from a magnetic tape or wire **c** to delete from a computer storage device **2 a** to remove from existence or memory as if by erasing **b** to nullify the effect or force of

It would have been impossible to (____)_____ the individual states.

4. **check** *n*

1 **a** a sudden stoppage of a forward course or progress: ARREST **b** a checking of an opposing player (as in ice hockey) **2** a sudden pause or break in a progression **3** one that arrests, limits, or restrains: RESTRAINT **4 a** a standard for testing and evaluation: CRITERION **b** EXAMINATION **c** INSPECTION, INVESTIGATION **5** a written order directing a bank to pay money as instructed

This system of government provides a (____)_____ on each branch by the other two.

• E. Information Organization

Read the article a second time. Underline what you think are the main ideas. Then scan the article and complete the following outline, using the sentences that you have underlined to help you. You will use this outline later to answer specific questions about the article.

I. The Origin of the Federal System of Government

   A.

   B. The Continental Congress existed, but had no legal power

   C. Legal governments in the states were established to replace colonial rule

   D.

II.

   A. Its purpose:

   B. The feelings of the writers of the Constitution:
     1.
     2. They did not want a strong central government
     3.
     4.

III.

   A. The purpose of this system:

     1.

     2.

     3.

   B. The powers not given to the government belong to the states

   C.

IV.

   A. The legislature, or Congress, drafts a law

   B.

   C.
     1.
     2.

   D. If someone challenges the law, the judicial branch determines whether the law is constitutional or not

• F. Information Organization Quiz and Summary

Read each question carefully. Use your notes to answer the questions. Do not refer back to the text. Write your answers in the space provided under each question. When you are finished, write a brief summary of the article.

1. a. What kind of government did the United States have before the Constitution was written?

   _____

   _____

   b. Was this government successful? Why, or why not?

   _____

   _____

2. What features of government didn't the writers of the Constitution want?

   _____

   _____

3. a. What is the purpose of the checks and balance system?

   _____

   _____

   b. How does it work?

   _____

   _____

   _____

4. How are laws made in the United States?

   _____

   _____

   _____

Summary

_____

_____

_____

_____

_____

• G. Critical Thinking Strategies

Read each question carefully. Write your response in the space provided. Remember that there is no one correct answer. Your response depends on what **you** think.

1. Read the first paragraph. Why does the article begin with a series of questions? In other words, what do you think is the author's purpose in asking the reader questions at the beginning of the reading passage?

   _____

   _____

   _____

   _____

2. Read lines 59–61. Why do you think these people were so sure about what kind of government they did *not* want?

   _____

   _____

   _____

   _____

3. Read the description of the checks and balance system in lines 77–132. Do you think that this system adequately protects the people's rights and that it prevents the federal government from becoming too powerful? Explain your answer.

   _____

   _____

   _____

   _____

4. Read lines 81–83: "A government ought to have three major powers: to make laws, to carry out those laws, and to provide justice under law for the best interests of the people." Do you agree or disagree with this statement? That is, do you think these should be the major powers of any government? Explain your answer.

   _____

   _____

   _____

   _____

5. After reading this selection, specifically lines 22–24, 62–67, and 93–97, what can you understand about the individuality of the states in the United States? For instance, how do you think that the fact that the United States is divided into states affects American culture and the attitudes of the people in each state?

_____

_____

_____

_____

• H. Follow-up Discussion and Activities

1. *Jigsaw Reading:* You are going to read about the three branches of the U.S. government: the legislative branch, the executive branch, and the judicial branch.

    a. First, read the paragraph entitled *The Checks and Balance System.* Discuss it in class to make sure everyone understands it.

    b. Second, work in a group of three or four students. Each group will read about one branch of government. Group A will read about the legislative branch, Group B will read about the executive branch, and Group C will read about the judicial branch. If your class is large, then you may have more than one Group A, B, or C; just make sure that at least one group reads about each branch of the government. After reading the paragraph, discuss it to make sure everyone in the group understands about their particular branch.

    c. Third, set up different groups so that each group has a student or students who have read about the three different branches. In these new groups, tell each other what you have read about each branch. Take notes about the other two readings. Do not look back at your readings. Ask each other questions to make sure that all the students in your group understand how the three branches work.

    d. Finally, work together to complete the Federal System of Government Chart on page 133. When your group is finished, compare your chart with the other groups' charts. You will use your chart to help you with the Library Resource assignments.

The Checks and Balance System

The writers of the Constitution wanted to make sure that the people's rights would always be safe and that the federal government would never become too powerful. Therefore, the writers of the Constitution set up three branches of government: the legislature, or Congress, to make laws; the executive branch—the president—to carry out the laws; the judicial branch, to watch over the rights of the people. The checks and balance system makes sure that one branch cannot become stronger than another. This system not only balances power among the three branches, but it also provides a check on each branch by the others.

GROUP A ONLY: *The Legislative Branch*

The legislative branch, or Congress, represents all states fairly. It consists of two parts: the House of Representatives and the Senate. The vice president of the United States acts as the president of the Senate. Each state has two senators, who are elected every six years. The number of members in the House of Representatives depends on the population of each state. Representatives are elected every two years. To be elected as a senator, a person must be at least 30 years old, have been a citizen for nine years, and be a resident of the state s/he will represent. To be elected as a representative, a person must be at least 25 years old, have been a citizen for seven years, and be a resident of the state s/he will represent.

The major job of the Congress is to make laws. If the president vetoes, or rejects, a proposed law, the Congress can pass the law anyway by getting a two-thirds majority vote. Congress can also declare war by getting a two-thirds majority vote of the senators and representatives. The House of Representatives can also impeach the president. This means that the House can charge the president with a crime. In this case, the Senate will put the president on trial, so the vice president must resign as the president of the Senate. The Senate votes to approve the justices that the president appoints to the Supreme Court. These are just a few of the legislative branch's many responsibilities.

Group B's Information:

_____

_____

_____

_____

_____

_____

Group C's Information:

_____

_____

_____

_____

_____

_____

GROUP B ONLY: *The Executive Branch*

The executive branch of the government puts the country's laws into effect. The president of the United States is a member of the executive branch. The president must be at least 35 years old, and be a natural citizen of the United States. In addition, he must have lived in the United States for at least 14 years, and be a civilian. The president is elected every four years and cannot serve more than two terms in a row. The vice president acts as president of the Senate. When the president receives a bill from Congress, he must sign it in order for it to become a law. However, if he disagrees with the law, he can veto, or reject, it. The president can also ask the Congress to declare war. He also appoints the justices to the Supreme Court. He must do his job according to the Constitution, or he may be impeached, that is, charged with a crime by Congress. The executive branch is a very important part of the U.S. government and must work with the other two branches according to the Constitution.

Group A's Information:

_____

_____

_____

_____

_____

_____

_____

_____

Group C's Information:

_____

_____

_____

_____

_____

_____

_____

_____

GROUP C ONLY: *The Judicial Branch*

The judicial branch of government is the system of courts in the United States. Its job is to enforce the laws. The Supreme Court is the highest court in the country. It consists of nine justices: one chief justice and eight associate justices. The Constitution does not state any specific requirements for Supreme Court positions. The president appoints the justices, but the Senate must approve them. The justices are appointed for life. The Supreme Court not only makes sure that people obey the laws, but can also declare a law unconstitutional. In other words, the Supreme Court can decide if a law is not in agreement with the Constitution. Furthermore, the chief justice acts as president of the Senate if there is an impeachment trial. In an impeachment trial, the Congress charges the president of the United States with a crime. The judicial branch works together with the legislative and executive branches to protect the Constitution and the rights of the people.

Group A's Information:

_____

_____

_____

_____

_____

_____

_____

Group B's Information:

_____

_____

_____

_____

_____

_____

_____

_____

• The Federal System of Government

1. In your groups, work together to complete the following chart. Do not look back to the paragraphs you have read.

	Legislative Branch	Executive Branch	Judicial Branch
Function			
Number of Members	Congress: _____Senators _____Representatives	1. 2. (acts as president of the Senate)	Justices: _____Chief Justice _____Associate Justices
Term of Office	Senate: House of Representatives:	President:	Justices:
Requirements	Senator: 1. 2. 3. 4. Representative: 1. 2.	President: 1. 2. 3. 4.	
Responsibilities : Laws	1. 2.	President: 1. 2. 3.	
Responsibilities: War		President:	
Impeachment	House of Representatives: Senate:	President: Vice President:	Chief Justice of the Supreme Court:

2. Alone, or with classmates from your country, write a description of the form of government in your country. Compare it with the form of government in the United States. For example, how are laws made? Who is the leader of the country? How is he or she granted this position? Compare your country's form of government with those of the other students' countries.

3. Is there something that the writers of the Constitution overlooked in the checks and balance system and that you think is important? In other words, did they forget to include a check or balance that you think is necessary to help control the federal government and keep it from becoming too powerful? Explain your answer.

• Library Resource Mastery

A federal system of government and a confederation are only two possible forms of government. For example, some countries have a parliamentary system; others have a monarchy. You are going to use the library to research one other form of government.

• Library Assignment

1. a. In class, list four or five of the possible forms of government. Divide the class into groups so that each group will research one of the forms of government you have listed.

   b. Go to the library. Use the card catalog to find a book or books on the form of government your group has chosen. Check the book out of the library.

   c. In class, use your books to describe the form of government your group is researching. Create a chart comparable to the U.S. Government chart.

   d. In class, form groups with the other students so that each group contains at least one student who has studied each form of government. Discuss your charts, and compare the features of each form of government. Make sure that each member of the group understands the different forms of government.

   e. Imagine that your group is a panel of experts. You have been selected as advisers to a newly established country to help establish a form of government that will be appropriate for that country and its people. Select one of the forms of government that your class has described, and present it to the representatives of the newly formed country. Give specific reasons why this particular form of government will be beneficial for the country. Discuss your decisions with your classmates.

2. The writers of the Constitution realized that it may need to be modified over the years, so they allowed for amendments to be made. However, to insure that these changes could not be made easily or quickly, they made the amendment process very complex. Go to the library, or refer to your history book. Find out how an amendment to the Constitution is made. Describe the process. How does this procedure help insure that power ultimately rests with the individual states and not the federal government?

Too Soon Old, Too Late Wise

by Evan Thomas with Adam Wolfberg
Newsweek

• Prereading Preparation

1. Look at the photographs of the two people on the left. Think about which one of these professors you would prefer to have as a teacher. Write down the reasons why you would choose one professor over the other. Compare your response with your classmates', and discuss whether the reasons people give are logical or emotional.
2. How old should a person be when he or she retires?
3. Should a person be required by law to retire at a certain age? Why, or why not?
4. In your country, must a person retire at a certain age? Why, or why not?
5. Work with a partner. Do you think there are some professions or jobs—e.g., police officers, airline pilots, etc.—from which people should retire at a specific age? Make a list of these jobs and the age at which people should retire from them. Discuss your list with your classmates.

1   The students of Prof. Paul Weiss at Catholic University
2 of America had to be careful about where they sat in his
3 classroom. Too far away from the podium and Professor
4 Weiss, who is a bit hard of hearing, might not catch their
5 questions. Too close and they risked getting an aimless
6 whack from his cane. But over the years the students kept
7 coming back because Weiss taught them to think. "He runs
8 the class by throwing out a series of theses. Then he basi-
9 cally says, 'Attack me,'" recalls a former student, Father
10 Robert Spitzer, 39, now a philosophy professor at Seattle
11 University.
12   Paul Weiss, 90, is a world-class philosopher, an emeri-
13 tus Sterling Professor at Yale and author of a score of

14 books. He was once regarded as a prize catch by Catholic
15 U., a financially pinched school of modest reputation in
16 Washington, D.C. But last summer Weiss was told that he
17 was being demoted to teaching graduate students part
18 time. The reason, according to the university, was "shifting
19 priorities." Weiss's highly personal brand of metaphysics
20 no longer suited the needs of the university's philosophy
21 department.

22   But the real reason that Weiss was shoved aside,
23 according to a report by the U.S. Equal Employment Oppor-
24 tunity Commission, was his age. When an EEOC investiga-
25 tor asked a university official what factors, other than his
26 salary and 20-year employment, went into the decision not
27 to renew his teaching contract, the official answered, "He's
28 90." Undergraduates should not be taught by someone like
29 "a grandfather," the official told the EEOC; Weiss should
30 make way "for a younger man." Earlier this month, the
31 EEOC gave Catholic a year to work out a settlement with
32 Weiss. If the university fails, the agency will sue for age
33 discrimination.

34   When is a teacher too old to teach? Airline pilots start
35 losing their reflexes as they age, and senility and infirmity
36 can be incapacitating in any profession. But philosophers
37 are supposed to just get wiser as they get older. Bertrand
38 Russell worked into his 90s, Kant into his 70s and Socrates
39 until he was about 70 and the Athenian tenure committee
40 chose not to renew his contract. Weiss believes he's an-
41 other wise man handed a goblet of hemlock. Weiss is deter-
42 mined to get his job back, even if it means a messy lawsuit.

43   Indeed, Weiss can't wait to go to court. A gnarled little
44 man who lurches about his book-filled apartment with the
45 aid of two canes, the professor loves confrontation. A high-
46 school dropout (his father was a tinsmith, his mother a
47 maid), Weiss took boxing lessons before going to night
48 school at City College of New York. In 1929 he took his
49 Ph.D. at Harvard. . . .Teaching philosophy at Yale in the late
50 '40s, Weiss was the first Jewish faculty member at Yale Col-
51 lege. . . .

52   **Not modest:** Father William Byron, Catholic's presi-
53 dent, insists that the university went out of its way to care
54 for Weiss. He says that Catholic allowed Weiss to teach stu-
55 dents out of his apartment after he was slowed down by a
56 back operation two years ago. Such an arrangement is "ab-
57 solutely unprecedented," Father Byron told *The Washing-*
58 *ton Post*. "False!" cries Professor Weiss. "Wittgenstein had

59 students come to his rooms at Cambridge," he declares.
60 "Alfred North Whitehead had students to his rooms at
61 Harvard. I know. I was one of them." Weiss is not modest
62 about the company he keeps. He also compares himself to
63 Plato ("who was out in left field, too"). In testifying before
64 the EEOC, Catholic administrators alluded to Weiss's "fad-
65 ing reputation." "Reputation!" exclaims Weiss. "*They* have
66 no reputation. I was in *Who's Who in the World*. They're not.
67 They teach philosophy. I'm a philosopher."

68   Weiss admits that he has a poor memory. For a scholar,
69 isn't that somewhat of a liability? "I've *always* had a bad
70 memory," he snaps. "I'm not haunted by what I know. I
71 think every issue afresh. A philosopher," he continues, "is
72 an arrogant man who asks himself fresh questions." Weiss
73 is delighted by the publicity his case has attracted. Colum-
74 nist William F. Buckley Jr., who studied under Weiss at
75 Yale, accused Catholic of "shabbily" treating a "truly emi-
76 nent" man. But Weiss was mildly offended when *The Wash-
77 ington Post* described him as a "manic lizard." "What are
78 they trying to convey by these references to reptiles?" he
79 asks a visiting journalist, who doesn't quite have the heart
80 to tell him that he looks like one. "That your movements
81 are quick?" the visitor suggests. "Hmm," he ponders.
82 "Makes sense." He raps his cane.

83   Weiss shows off his latest manuscript, "Being and Other
84 Realities," 500 pages of typescript covered with changes in
85 black ink. "Revise! Revise!" he growls. "I am constantly re-
86 vising." He works on the book from morning until night but
87 says he misses his students. "I cherish teaching," he says.
88 "When will he be ready to give it up?" "When I'm vague and
89 puttering," he barks, in a tone that defies anyone to sug-
90 gest that he is either.

• A. Fact-Finding Exercise

Read the passage once. Then read the following statements. Scan the article quickly to find out if each statement is true (T) or false (F). If a statement is false, change it so that it is true.

_____ T _____F   1. Prof. Paul Weiss teaches philosophy at Catholic University.

_____

_____ T _____F   2. Officials at Catholic University believe that Prof. Weiss is too old to teach.

_____

_____ T _____F   3. Prof. Paul Weiss wants to stop teaching because of his age.

_____

_____ T _____F   4. Prof. Weiss does not want to go to court to settle his problem with the university.

_____

_____ T _____F   5. Prof. Weiss studied at Yale College.

_____

_____ T _____F   6. This situation has attracted a lot of publicity.

_____

• B. Reading Analysis

Read each question carefully. Circle the number or letter of the correct answer, or write your answer in the space provided.

1. In lines 3–5, **a bit hard of hearing** means:
   a. a little confusing.
   b. a little difficult.
   c. a little deaf.

2. Read lines 7–8: "He **runs** the class by throwing out a series of theses." This sentence means
   a. he walks quickly in the class.
   b. he asks the class.
   c. he teaches the class.

3. In lines 13–14, what is a **score of books**?
   a. many books
   b. a few books
   c. a type of book

4. Read lines 16–18. What does **demoted** mean?
   a. given a better job
   b. given a less important job
   c. given a new job

5. Read lines 18 and 19. Why is "**shifting priorities**" in quotation marks?
   a. to provide emphasis
   b. because the author disagrees
   c. because it is a direct quote

6. Read lines 22–28. What is the EEOC?

   _____

7. Read lines 29 and 30: "Weiss should make way 'for a younger man.'" This statement means that
   a. Weiss should let a younger man have his job.
   b. Weiss should help younger students find jobs.
   c. Weiss should give his office to a younger man.

8. Read lines 34–36. **As they age** means
   a. as they reach a specific age.
   b. as they get older.
   c. as they work hard.

9. Read lines 36–40.
   a. Who are the people referred to here?

   _____

   b. How do you know?

   _____

10. Read line 43: "Indeed, Weiss can't wait to go to court." This sentence means that
    a. Weiss wants to go to court.
    b. Weiss doesn't want to go to court.

11. Read lines 45–48. What is Prof. Weiss' family background?
    a. His parents were wealthy and well educated.
    b. His parents were wealthy but poorly educated.
    c. His parents were poor and poorly educated.
    d. His parents were poor but well educated.

12. Refer to lines 48–51. What is the purpose of the ellipses (. . .)?
    a. to show emphasis
    b. to indicate that text has been deleted
    c. to show direct speech

13. Read lines 52–61.
    a. **Unprecedented** describes something that
       1. happens all the time.
       2. has never happened before.
       3. is not permitted to happen.

    b. In line 61, who does **them** refer to?

    _____

14. Read lines 63–66.
    a. Who does **they** refer to?

    _____

    b. Why is **they** in italics?

    _____

15. Read lines 68–70.
    a. What is a **liability**?
       1. an advantage
       2. a disadvantage
       3. a danger

    b. What might be a liability to a teacher?

    _____

• C. Word Forms

Part 1

In English, some adjectives become nouns by adding the suffix *-ity*, for example, *real* (adj.), *reality* (n.).

Complete each sentence with the correct form of the words on the left.

equal (adj.)
equality (n.)

1. a. In the United States, the Constitution guarantees everyone _____ rights under the law.

   b. This guarantee of _____ was written over two hundred years ago.

infirm (adj.)
infirmity (n.)

2. a. Prof. Weiss does not consider his age to be an _____. He feels capable of teaching, even at 90.

   b. In other words, Prof. Weiss is 90 years old, but he is by no means _____.

public (adj.)
publicity (n.)

3. a. The lives of politicians and actors are always exposed to a lot of _____.

   b. However, some people do not always like having their private lives under _____ scrutiny, or examination.

senile (adj.)
senility (n.)

4. a. Contrary to popular myth, _____ is not an inevitable part of becoming older.

   b. In fact, most older people never become at all _____. Their minds remain sharp and clear.

anxious (adj.)
anxiety (n.)

5. a. Michael invariably experiences intense _____ right before taking an important exam.

   b. Because he tends to become so _____, he has begun doing special exercises to help him relax.

Part 2

In English, some verbs become nouns by adding the suffix *-ance* or *-ence*, for example, *insist* (v.), *insistence* (n.).

Complete each sentence with the correct form of the words on the left. **Use the correct tense of the verbs in either the affirmative or the negative form. Use the singular or plural form of the nouns.**

defy (v.)
defiance (n.)

1. a. Eleanor _____ her parents' authority and stayed out until after midnight last Friday.

    b. Because of her open _____ of established rules, her parents grounded her for two weeks. In other words, she cannot go out on evenings or weekends for two weeks.

disturb (v.)
disturbance (n.)

2. a. Please _____ us for a few hours. I've just put the baby to sleep, and I need to take a nap, too.

    b. If you make any _____, she will wake up and begin to cry, and neither of us will get any rest.

insist (v.)
insistence (n.)

3. a. I don't understand your _____ on always eating dinner at home.

    b. Tonight, I absolutely _____ that we go out to a restaurant for dinner. It'll be my treat, too.

refer (v.)
reference (n.)

4. a. Gene didn't do well on his history paper because he _____ to any sources for his information.

    b. His history professor told him to rewrite the paper and to give several _____ in a bibliography.

insure (v.)
insurance (n.)

5. a. Connie made extra copies of her house keys and gave them to me as a sort of _____.

    b. If she loses them, she still _____ that she won't be locked out of her apartment.

• D. Dictionary Skills

Choose the appropriate definition for each word. Then write the number and the synonym or meaning in the space provided. Remember that you may need to change the wording of the definition in order to have a grammatically correct sentence.

1. **messy** *adj*   **1** marked by confusion, disorder, or dirt: UNTIDY **2** lacking neatness or precision: CARELESS, SLOVENLY **3** extremely unpleasant or trying

    Weiss is determined to get his job back, even if it means a(n)

    (____) _____ lawsuit.

2. **declare** *v*   **1** to make known formally or explicitly   **2** to make evident: SHOW   **3** to state emphatically: AFFIRM **4** to make a full statement of (one's taxable or dutiable property)

    Prof. Weiss (____) _____ that Alfred North Whitehead had stu-

    dents come to his rooms at Harvard. He was one of those students.

3. **case** *n*   **1 a** a set of circumstances or conditions   **b** (1) a situation requiring investigation or action (as by the police) (2) the object of investigation or consideration **2** CONDITION: *specif*: condition of body or mind **3** an inflectional form of a noun, pronoun, or adjective indicating its grammatical relation to other words **4 a** a suit or action in law or equity   **b** the evidence supporting a conclusion or judgment   **5** an instance of disease or injury

    Prof. Weiss is delighted by the publicity his (____) _____ has

    attracted.

4. **vague** *adj*   **1 a** not clearly expressed: stated in indefinite terms **b** not having a precise meaning   **2 a** not clearly defined, grasped, or understood: INDISTINCT   **b** not clearly felt or sensed   **3** not thinking or expressing one's thoughts clearly or precisely   **4** not sharply outlined: HAZY

    Prof. Weiss said that he will give up teaching when he becomes a per-

    son who is (____) _____.

• E. Information Organization

Read the article a second time. Underline what you think are the main ideas. Then scan the article and complete the following flowchart, using the sentences that you have underlined to help you. You will use this flowchart later to answer specific questions about the article.

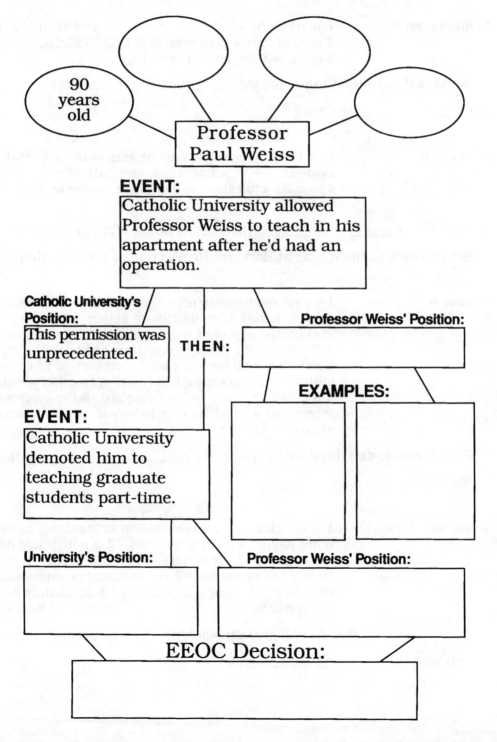

• F. Information Organization Quiz and Summary

Read each question carefully. Use your notes to answer the questions. Do not refer back to the text. Write your answers in the space provided under each question. When you are finished, write a brief summary of the article.

1. Describe Prof. Paul Weiss.

   _____

   _____

2. a. What did Catholic University do after Prof. Weiss had an operation?

   _____

   _____

   b. What did Catholic University say about this?

   _____

   _____

   c. What did Prof. Weiss say about this?

   _____

   _____

3. a. What did Catholic University do next?

   _____

   _____

   b. According to Catholic University, why did it do this?

   _____

   _____

   c. What does Prof. Weiss want to do about this situation?

   _____

   _____

4. What is the EEOC's decision about this situation?

   _____

   _____

   _____

Summary

_____

_____

_____

_____

_____

• G. Critical Thinking Strategies

Read each question carefully. Write your response in the space provided. Remember that there is no one correct answer. Your response depends on what **you** think.

1. Read lines 6–11. What do you think is Prof. Weiss' approach to teaching?

   _____

   _____

   _____

   _____

2. Read lines 52–67. How does this paragraph make clear that Prof. Weiss is not a modest man?

   _____

   _____

   _____

   _____

3. *Who's Who in the World* is a book that lists internationally notable people and gives a brief biography of each one. Read lines 66–67. Few teachers are listed in this book. What do you think this fact tells you about Prof. Weiss?

   _____

   _____

   _____

   _____

4. What do you think the author's opinion of Dr. Weiss's situation is? Does the author believe Dr. Weiss should be forced to retire? Why do you think so?

_____

_____

_____

_____

• H. Follow-up Discussion and Activities

1. What type of person do you think Prof. Paul Weiss is? Describe the characteristics of Weiss's personality. For example, is he friendly? patient? intelligent? Write a composition and give examples from the article for your description.

2. In your country, are there laws that require people to retire at a certain age? What are these laws? Do you agree with these laws? Why, or why not? Explain your answer.

3. In the United States, the Equal Employment Opportunity Commission (EEOC) does not allow employers to discriminate against older people. In other words, a person's age cannot be considered when an employer makes decisions about hiring, promoting, or firing employees. Do you agree with this policy? Why, or why not?

The Pursuit of Excellence

by Jill Smolowe
Time

• Prereading Preparation

1. In your country, what are the requirements for a student to attend college? Can any student go to college in your country? Why, or why not?
2. In the United States, what are the requirements for a foreign student to attend college? What are the requirements for an American student to attend college? Can any student go to college?
3. Why did you come to another country to study? Why do you think there are so many foreign students in American universities?
4. Take an in-class survey of the reasons students decide to study in another country.
   a. In small groups, discuss why students might choose to study abroad, e.g., cost, choice of subjects, etc.
   b. In your group, list the reasons you decided to study abroad.
   c. Compare your list with the other groups' lists. What is the most common reason students in your class have for studying abroad? The second most common reason? The third? Save your lists. Later, you will use these to compare to the responses from the survey you will do.
5. Look at the title of this article. What do you think it means?

1   Sometime around the seventh grade, many American
2 students are introduced to the tale of 10 blind men in-
3 specting an elephant. When each blind man reaches differ-
4 ent conclusions about the creature, the students are
5 invited to consider whether truth is absolute or lies in the
6 eye of the beholder. College professors and administrators
7 might want to remember that fable when they take the
8 measure of American higher education. Many of them, who
9 tend to see only what they stand to lose, perceive the beast

10 as wounded, suffering from the shocks of rising costs,
11 dwindling resources and life-draining cutbacks. But for-
12 eigners, who compare America's universities with their
13 own, often reach very different conclusions about the na-
14 ture of the beast.
15   If sheer numbers provide any proof, America's univer-
16 sities and colleges are the envy of the world. For all their
17 abiding troubles, the United States' 3,500 institutions were
18 flooded with 407,530 students from 193 different coun-
19 tries last year. Asia led the way with 39,600 students from
20 China and 36,610 from Japan, followed by India and
21 Canada. Many of the foreigners entered graduate and un-
22 dergraduate programs in roughly equal numbers. . . .
23   Most European and Asian universities provide an elite
24 service to a small and privileged clientele. While fully 60%
25 of all U.S. high school graduates attend college at some
26 point in their life, just 30% of the comparable German
27 population, 28% of the French, 20% of the British and 37%
28 of the Japanese proceed beyond high school. German stu-
29 dents who survive the Abitur or Britons who pass their A
30 levels may still not qualify for a top university at home,
31 but find American universities far more welcoming. Some
32 U.S. schools acknowledge the rigor of European secondary
33 training and will give up to a year's credit to foreigners
34 who have passed their high school exams.
35   "The egalitarian conception that everyone has a right to
36 an education appropriate to his potential is a highly demo-
37 cratic and compassionate standard," says Marvin Bressler,
38 professor of sociology and education specialist at Prince-
39 ton University. True, not all U.S. collegians can match the
40 performance of their foreign counterparts, but American
41 institutions do offer students from rich and poor families
42 alike the chance to realize their full potential. "America
43 educates so many more people at university that one can't
44 expect all those who go to be either as well informed or in-
45 telligent as the much narrower band who go to English uni-
46 versities," says Briton Christopher Ricks, professor of
47 English at Boston University. Having instructed at Cam-
48 bridge, Ricks knows that teaching T. S. Eliot to British un-
49 dergraduates is an easier task. Yet he finds teaching at B.U.
50 very rewarding. "I'm not against elitism," he says, "But I
51 happen to like having people who are more eager to learn."
52   The democratic impulse to reach out to so many first
53 took seed after World War II, when the G.I. bill made fund-
54 ing for higher education available to all returning soldiers.

55 As universities expanded to handle the sudden influx, they
56 developed the flexibility that has become one of the hall-
57 marks of American higher learning. "In the U.S. there is a
58 system of infinite chances," says Diane Ravitch, Assistant
59 Secretary of Education. "At 35, you can decide to go back to
60 college, upgrade your education, change your profession."
61   While Americans take such flexibility for granted, for-
62 eigners do not. To French students, who are commonly ex-
63 pected at age 16 to select both a university and a specific
64 course of study, the American practice of jumping not only
65 from department to department but also from school to
66 school seems a luxury. Japanese students find it all but
67 impossible to transfer credits from one school to another.
68 Thus students who initially enter a junior college and sub-
69 sequently decide to earn a bachelor's degree must head
70 overseas.
71   Many are attracted not only to the academic programs
72 at a particular U.S. college but also to the larger commu-
73 nity, which affords the chance to soak up the surrounding
74 culture. Few foreign universities put much emphasis on
75 the cozy communal life that characterizes American cam-
76 puses: from clubs and sports teams to student publica-
77 tions and theatrical societies. "The campus and the
78 American university have become identical in people's
79 minds," says Brown University President Vartan Gregorian.
80 "In America it is assumed that a student's daily life is as
81 important as his learning experience. . . ."
82   Foreign students also come in search of choices.
83 America's menu of options—research universities, state
84 institutions, private liberal-arts schools, community col-
85 leges, religious institutions, military academies—is unri-
86 valed. "In Europe," says history professor Jonathan
87 Steinberg, who has taught at both Harvard and Cambridge,
88 "there is one system, and that is it." While students over-
89 seas usually must demonstrate expertise in a single field,
90 whether law or philosophy or chemistry, most American
91 universities insist that students sample natural and social
92 sciences, languages and literature before choosing a field
93 of concentration.
94   Such opposing philosophies grow out of different tradi-
95 tions and power structures. In Europe and Japan universi-
96 ties are answerable only to a Ministry of Education, which
97 sets academic standards and distributes money. While cen-
98 tralization ensures that all students are equipped with
99 roughly the same resources and perform at roughly the

100 same level, it also discourages experimentation. "When
101 they make mistakes, they make big ones," says Robert
102 Rosenzweig, president of the Association of American Uni-
103 versities. "They set a system in wrong directions, and it's
104 like steering a supertanker."
105   U.S. colleges, on the other hand, are so responsive to
106 cultural currents that they are often on the cutting edge of
107 social change. Such sensitivity—some might argue hyper-
108 sensitivity—to the culture around them reflects the broad
109 array of constituencies to which college administrators
110 must answer. The board of trustees, composed of commu-
111 nity and national leaders, serves as a referee between the
112 institutional culture and the surrounding community;
113 alumni and corporate donors, who often earmark monies
114 for specific expenditures; student bodies that demand a
115 voice in university life; legislators who apportion govern-
116 ment funds; and an often feisty faculty.
117   Smaller colleges are particularly attractive to foreign
118 students because they are likely to offer direct contact
119 with professors. "We have one of the few systems in the
120 world where students are actually expected to go to class,"
121 says Rosenzweig. With the exception of Britain, where
122 much of the teaching takes place in one-on-one tutorials,
123 European students rarely come into direct contact with
124 professors until they reach graduate-level studies. Even
125 lectures are optional in Europe, since students are graded
126 solely on examinations, with no eye to class attendance or
127 participation. . . .
128   In some respects, the independent spirit of the Ameri-
129 can university that foreigners admire comes down to dol-
130 lars and cents. All U.S. colleges, private and public alike,
131 must fight vigorously to stay alive. They compete not only
132 for students but also for faculty and research grants. Such
133 competition, though draining and distracting, can stimu-
134 late creativity and force administrators to remain attentive
135 to student needs. "U.S. students pay for their education,"
136 says Ulrich Littmann, head of the German Fulbright Com-
137 mission, "and demand a commensurate value for what
138 they—or their parents—pay."
139   Most universities abroad have state funding, but that
140 luxury has a steep price: universities have less opportunity
141 to develop distinctive personalities and define distinctive
142 personalities and define their own missions. . . .

143 If the financial crisis besetting U.S. campuses is mis-
144 handled, Americans may discover they don't know what
145 they've got until it's gone. "By the year 2000, American
146 higher education will no longer be dominant in the world,"
147 warns Joseph Duffey, president of American University in
148 Washington. "Our general belief in education and our abil-
149 ity to finance it are running out. . . ."

• A. Fact-Finding Exercise

Read the passage once. Then read the following statements. Scan the article quickly to find out if each statement is true (T) or false (F). If a statement is false, change it so that it is true.

_____ T _____ F 1. Most foreign students in American universities come from Canada.

_____ T _____ F 2. Most U.S. high school graduates go to college.

_____ T _____ F 3. Foreign students attend U.S. universities only for educational reasons.

_____ T _____ F 4. Students in American universities must take a variety of courses in addition to courses in their major field.

_____ T _____ F 5. In an American university, it is not likely that students will be in direct contact with their teachers.

_____ T _____ F 6. Many American universities today are having financial problems.

• B. Reading Analysis

Read each question carefully. Circle the number or letter of the correct answer, or write your answer in the space provided.

1. Read the first paragraph. What do college professors and administrators believe about American universities?
   a. American universities are superior to foreign universities.
   b. There is a financial crisis in American universities.
   c. They think that American universities are very expensive.

2. Read lines 19–21. "Asia led the way with 39,600 students from China and 36,610 from Japan, followed by India and Canada." This statement means
   a. Asian students arrived first.
   b. Chinese students were in front of Japanese students.
   c. more students came from Asia than from anywhere else.
   d. Indian students followed Japanese students.

3. Read lines 21–22. This statement means
   a. half of foreign students entered undergraduate school and half entered graduate school.
   b. more foreign students entered undergraduate school than graduate school.

4. Read lines 23 and 24. Which word is a synonym of **elite**?

   _____

5. Read lines 24–28.
   a. **At some point in their life** means that most U.S. high school graduates
      1. enter college at the same age.
      2. enter college before they get married.
      3. enter college at different times.
   b. What is the **comparable German population**?
      1. German high school graduates
      2. German college students
      3. German people

6. Read lines 28–31.
   a. What are the **Arbitur** and the **A levels**?

   _____

   b. How do you know?

   _____

7. Read lines 31–34.

   a. This statement means that
      1. European secondary training is more difficult than American secondary training.
      2. American secondary training is more difficult than European secondary training.

   b. **Secondary training** refers to
      1. graduate school.
      2. college.
      3. high school.

8. Read lines 39–42.

   a. **Counterparts** refers to
      1. foreign college students.
      2. American college students.
      3. rich students.
      4. poor students.

   b. **Rich and poor families alike** means
      1. rich families are like poor families.
      2. both rich families *and* poor families.
      3. rich families and poor families like each other.

9. Read lines 57–60. **Chances** means
   a. risks.
   b. opportunities.
   c. accidents.

10. Read lines 62–66. **Jumping from department to department** means
    a. taking gymnastics classes.
    b. changing universities.
    c. changing majors.

11. Read lines 66–70.

    a. **All but impossible** means
       1. completely impossible.
       2. almost impossible.
       3. everything is impossible.

    b. **Thus** means
       1. afterwards.
       2. in addition.
       3. as a result.

    c. **Initially** means
      1. first.
      2. second.
      3. third.

    d. **Subsequently** means
      1. first
      2. next
      3. last

12. Read lines 82–86.

    a. Which words are synonyms of **choice**?

    _____

    b. What is between the dashes (—)?
      1. new information about options.
      2. examples of options.
      3. contrasting information.

13. Read lines 117–127.

    a. This statement means that students in European classes
      1. never attend classes.
      2. must attend classes.
      3. do not have to attend classes.

    b. **Optional** means
      1. necessary.
      2. not necessary.
      3. important.

14. Read lines 139–142. What follows the colon (:)?
    a. the cost of state funding
    b. an explanation of the price
    c. a description of universities

15. In lines 22, 81, and elsewhere there are ellipses (. . .) at the end of
    the paragraph. These dots indicate that
    a. the last sentence is incomplete.
    b. text has been deleted from the article.
    c. there are exactly three sentences missing.

• C. Word Forms

Part 1

In English, some adjectives become nouns by adding the suffix *-ity*, for example, *fatal* (adj.), *fatality* (n.).

Complete each sentence with the correct form of the words on the left. **Use the singular or plural form of the nouns.**

individual (adj.)
individuality (n.)

1. a. Even though they may be in a large class, students like to receive _____ treatment from their teachers.
   b. Everyone likes to preserve their _____, even if they are part of a large group.

creative (adj.)
creativity (n.)

2. a. People can demonstrate _____ in many ways.
   b. For instance, some people have _____ ways of expressing themselves in words, others in decorating their homes, still others in painting or photography.

diverse (adj.)
diversity (n.)

3. a. In a typical ESL classroom, you will find students from a wide _____ of countries.
   b. In fact, even if students are from the same country, they may come from _____ backgrounds.

national (adj.)
nationality (n.)

4. a. Each country has its own _____ anthem, or song.
   b. There are students of very different _____ in this class.

flexible (adj.)
flexibility (n.)

5. a. There is considerable _____ in this English program.
   b. For example, the days and the hours of classes are quite _____.

Part 2

In English, some adjectives become nouns by deleting the final *-t* and adding *-ce*, for example, *negligent* (adj.), *negligence* (n.).

Complete each sentence with the correct form of the words on the left.

independent (adj.)

independence (n.)

1. a. In the past several years, many countries have struggled for and gained their.

    b. These newly _____ countries usually have to contend with many difficulties as they try to maintain stability.

different (adj.)

difference (n.)

2. a. I haven't noticed any _____ in the quality of the food in this restaurant since they hired a new cook last week.

    b. The meals don't taste any _____ than they did last month.

dominant (adj.)

dominance (n.)

3. a. According to geneticists, brown eyes are always _____ over blue eyes.

    b. This _____ means that if one parent has brown eyes and the other parent has blue eyes, the children will most likely have brown eyes.

excellent (adj.)

excellence (n.)

4. a. We all strive for _____, and sometimes we achieve it.

    b. Even if everything we do isn't always _____, we can always try harder the next time.

important (adj.)

importance (n.)

5. a. The students want to know how much _____ the teacher is going to give to their homework.

    b. In other words, they want to know how _____ the homework is to their grade.

• D. Dictionary Skills

Choose the appropriate definition for each word. Then write the number and the synonym or meaning in the space provided. Remember that you may need to change the wording of the definition in order to have a grammatically correct sentence.

1. **roughly** *adv*　　1 in a rough manner: as **a** with harshness or violence **b** in crude fashion: IMPERFECTLY　2 without completeness or exactness: APPROXIMATELY

Many of the foreigners entered graduate and undergraduate programs in (＿＿) ＿＿＿＿＿ equal numbers.

2. **match** *v*　　1 **a** to set in competition or opposition　**b** to set in comparison　2 to join or give in marriage　3 **a** to cause to correspond: SUIT　**b** to be the counterpart of; *also*, to compare favorably with　4 to fit together or make suitable for fitting together

Not all U.S. collegians can (＿＿) ＿＿＿＿＿ the performance of their foreign counterparts.

3. **practice** *n*　　1 **a** actual performance or application　**b** a repeated or customary action　**c** the usual way of doing something　**d** the form, manner, and order of conducting legal suits and prosecutions　2 **a** a systematic exercise for proficiency　**b** the condition of being proficient through systematic exercise　3 the continuous exercise of a profession

The American (＿＿) ＿＿＿＿＿ of jumping from department to department seems a luxury.

4. **demonstrate** *v*　　1 to show clearly　2 **a** to prove or make clear by reasoning or evidence　**b** to illustrate and explain esp. with many examples　3 to show or prove the value or efficiency of to a prospective buyer

Students overseas must (＿＿) ＿＿＿＿＿ expertise in a single field, whether law or philosophy or chemistry.

• E. Information Organization

Read the article a second time. Underline what you think are the main ideas. Then scan the article and complete the following chart, using the sentences that you have underlined to help you. You will use this chart later to answer specific questions about the article. Not all the boxes will be filled in.

	the United States	*Japan*	Europe
Percent of high school graduates who attend college			
Differences between universities (freedom of choice)	1. 2. 3.	1.	France: 1.
Differences in types of colleges	1.		1.
Funding for education	1.	1.	1.

• F. Information Organization Quiz and Summary

Read each question carefully. Use your notes to answer the questions. Do not refer back to the text. Write your answers in the space provided under each question. When you are finished, write a brief summary of the article.

1. a. What percent of U.S. high school graduates enter college?

   _____

   b. What percent of high school graduates enter college in countries in Europe and Asia?

   _____

   _____

2. What are some differences between universities in the United States and those in Europe and in Asia?

   _____

   _____

   _____

3. How are colleges in the United States different financially from colleges in other countries?

   _____

   _____

   _____

Summary

_____

_____

_____

_____

• G. Critical Thinking Strategies

Read each question carefully. Write your response in the space provided. Remember that there is no one correct answer. Your response depends on what **you** think.

1. In lines 77–81, Brown University President Gregorian says, "In America it is assumed that a student's daily life is as important as his learning experience." From this statement, what expectations, other than academic, can we assume that American universities have of all their students, including foreign students?

   _____

   _____

   _____

   _____

2. Read lines 90–93. Why do you think American universities have these requirements?

   _____

   _____

   _____

   _____

3. In lines 128–138, the author discusses the money factor. What connection does she make between paying for one's education and the university's responsibility to its students?

   _____

   _____

   _____

   _____

4. Read lines 139–142. What do you think the author believes is the effect of state funding on foreign universities?

   _____

   _____

   _____

   _____

5. Read the last paragraph in the article. The author shifts suddenly from her focus on foreign students in American universities to a warning regarding the financial crisis affecting U.S. campuses. Why do you think the author made this unexpected change? What other purpose might she have had in writing this article besides comparing American and foreign universities?

_____

_____

_____

_____

6. Think about how the author presented the information in this article.

   a. Do you think she was objective or subjective in describing the American university system? Why do you think so? Refer to specific sentences in the reading to support your opinion.

   _____

   _____

   _____

   _____

   b. Do you think she was objective or subjective in describing foreign students? Why do you think so? Refer to specific sentences in the reading to support your opinion.

   _____

   _____

   _____

   _____

• H. Follow-up Discussion and Activities

1. Refer back to the chart in Exercise E. Choose two differences between American universities and foreign universities. Using the
   following chart, write the differences you have chosen and list
   what you think the advantages and disadvantages are. Compare
   your chart with your classmates' charts.

	in the United States	in Japan	in Europe
	1.	1.	1.
Advantages			
Disadvantages			
	2.	2.	2.
Advantages			
Disadvantages			

2. a. Refer to the College Survey below. As a class, add more reasons to #5 in order to complete the survey.

   b. After you have finished the questionnaire, go outside your class alone or in pairs. Survey two or three international students. Then bring back your data and combine it with the other students' information. How do your results compare with the results you obtained in your class? Do you think that international students have similar reasons for studying in another country? What are the main reasons you discovered, in both your in-class and your out-of-class surveys?

College Survey

The purpose of this questionnaire is to collect data regarding students' reasons for studying in a foreign country.

1. Interviewee is ___ Male ___ Female
   Please answer the following questions.

2. What country are you from?
   _____

3. What field do you plan to major in?
   _____

4. Are you going to enter an undergraduate program or a graduate program?
   _____

5. Why did you choose to study in the United States? Please indicate all the reasons that apply.

   _____ cost of education   *Other Reasons*

   _____ improve my English   _____

   _____ get away from home   _____

   _____ choice of courses   _____

   _____ study my major   _____

6. Read the reasons you have indicated for studying in the United States. Put them in order of importance. That is, write **1** next to your most important reason, **2** next to the second most important reason, etc.

3. Describe your experience as a foreign student in the United States, or the experience of someone you know who has studied in the United States. What was positive about the experience? What was negative about the experience? Explain.

4. Work with one or two partners. List the potential difficulties of being a foreign student in the United States. Discuss how you can deal with these problems to reduce or eliminate them.

5. One problem that foreign students frequently encounter is loneliness and difficulty making friends. Work with a partner. Plan several strategies for reducing loneliness and making friends.

6. Imagine that a friend wants to come to the United States to study. Write your friend a letter. Tell him or her what to expect as a foreign student and how to prepare before leaving home.

• Library Resource Mastery

Go to the Reference section of the library, or ask the librarian where college bulletins are located.

1. a. Get a college bulletin for the college or university that you are attending or plan to attend. Read through the introduction and course requirements for your major.

   b. How are these requirements different from what you expected? Write a composition describing the differences and how you plan to handle these differences.

Unit III Review

• I. Vocabulary Categorization

The words in the vocabulary list below have been taken from the three readings in this unit. Read through the list, and place the words into the three categories indicated. Write in the appropriate heading for the category that has been left blank. Remember, a word may fit into more than one category.

arrogance	government	philosophy
authority	independence	power
competition	individuality	pride
Congress	innovator	privilege
creativity	justice	reputation
decisions	liability	rule
democracy	liberty	scholar
excellence	majority	system
finance	options	testimony
flexibility	participation	vigilance

Personality Traits	**Law**	_____

• J. Crossword Puzzle

Across

1. A problem with no perfect solution
7. Negative feelings or actions against a person
10. Am, is, _____
11. A privileged group is an _____ group.
12. Some people believe that old age is a _____—a disadvantage.
13. Remember
15. _____ are important things, listed in their order of importance.
19. Choices; rights
20. The opposite of **out**
21. Capability; possibility
23. _____, subtract, multiply, divide
25. A _____ is a legal action against someone.
26. A _____ consists of more than half of a group.
28. A democracy is one possible _____ of government.
30. The opposite of **lose**
31. North, south, east, _____

Down

1. The past of **do**
2. High quality; superiority
3. Your hand is at the end of your _____.
4. A _____ is a presidential refusal to sign a bill into law.
5. A person's _____ is the opinion that other people generally have of him or her.
6. Something that has never happened before is _____.
8. Your _____ of something is based on your observation and understanding of it.
9. When you give people a job, you _____, or employ, them.
14. The Congress is also called the _____ because its function is to make laws.
16. An _____ is something new that is introduced.
17. Prof. Weiss is _____ young; he is 90 years old.
18. Move into action; activate; energize
22. At the present time
24. Protect
25. The opposite of **first**
27. The opposite of **on**
29. I, _____; he, him

Unit IV

Science and Technology

Atlantic Ocean

EUROPE

AFRICA

Indian Ocean

NORTH & SOUTH AMERICA

ANTARCTICA

ASIA

South Pole

Ross Ice Shelf

Pacific Ocean

AUSTRALIA

Antarctica:
Whose Continent Is It Anyway?

by Daniel and Sally Grotta
Popular Science

• Prereading Preparation

1. Where is **Antarctica**?
2. Work with a partner. Discuss what you know about Antarctica, and fill in the chart below with your information.

Climate	Geography	People	Animals	Plants

3. Some scientists want to study Antarctica. What are some reasons why?
4. Look at the title. What do you think this article will discuss?

1   Last February the *World Discoverer*, our cruise ship,
2 stopped in front of a white ice cliff higher than the ship's
3 mast. As large as France, the Ross Ice Shelf of Antarctica
4 extends unbroken along the Ross Sea for hundreds of
5 miles.
6   Like other passengers on our cruise ship, we had been
7 lured by an irresistible attraction: the chance to visit the
8 most remote place on Earth, and the most unusual. The
9 coldest place on Earth is also the subject of conflicting in-
10 terests: Scientists, tourists, environmentalists, oil and min-
11 eral seekers.
12   Scientists treasure the unparalleled advantages for re-
13 search; tourists prize the chance to visit Earth's last fron-
14 tier; environmentalists fear that increases in both activities
15 will pollute the continent and jeopardize its fabulous crea-

16 tures; others contend that preserving Antarctica as a kind
17 of world park will deprive the rest of the world of much
18 needed oil and mineral reserves.
19   Fears of Antarctica's ruin through commercial exploita-
20 tion have been partly reduced by the October, 1991 31-na-
21 tion signing of the Madrid Protocol, which bans oil and gas
22 exploration for the next 50 years. But Antarctica's unique
23 attributes—it is the coldest, driest, and highest continent—
24 will keep it at the focus of conflicting scientific and touris-
25 tic interests.
26   Think of a place as remote as the far side of the moon,
27 as strange as Saturn and as inhospitable as Mars, and that
28 will give some idea of what Antarctica is like. A mere 2.4
29 percent of its 5.4 million-square-mile land mass is ice-free,
30 and, then, only for a few months a year. Scientists estimate
31 that 70 percent of the world's fresh water is locked away in
32 Antarctica's icecap; if it were ever to melt, sea levels might
33 rise 200 feet. In Antarctica, winds can blow at better than
34 200 mph, and temperatures drop as low as minus 128.6˚F.
35 There's not a single village or town, not a tree, bush, or
36 blade of grass on the entire continent.
37   But far from being merely a useless continent, Antarc-
38 tica is vital to life on Earth. The continent's vast ice fields
39 reflect sunlight back into space, preventing the planet from
40 overheating. The cold water that the breakaway icebergs
41 generate flows north and mixes with equatorial warm wa-
42 ter, producing currents, clouds, and ultimately creating
43 complex weather patterns. Antarctic seas teem with life,
44 making them an important link in the world food chain.
45 The frigid waters of the Southern Ocean are home to spe-
46 cies of birds and mammals that are found nowhere else.
47   The National Science Foundation (NSF) is the govern-
48 ment agency responsible for the U.S. stations in Antarctica.
49 Because of the continent's extreme cold and almost com-
50 plete isolation, the NSF considers it to be the best place to
51 study and understand such phenomena as tempera-
52 ture circulation in the oceans, unique animal life, ozone
53 depletion, and glacial history. And buried deep in layers of
54 Antarctic ice lie clues to ancient climates, clues such as
55 trapped bubbles of atmospheric gases, which can help pre-
56 dict whether present and future global warming poses a
57 real threat.
58   Until scientists began the first serious study of the con-
59 tinent during the 1957–'58 International Geophysical Year

60 (IGY), a multi-country cooperative research project, Antarc-
61 tica was dismissed as a vast, useless continent.
62   Based upon early explorations and questionable land
63 grants, seven countries, including Great Britain, Chile, and
64 Argentina, claim sovereignty over vast tracts of the conti-
65 nent. However, as IGY wound down, the question of who
66 owns Antarctica came to a head. The 12 participating coun-
67 tries reached an international agreement, the Antarctic
68 Treaty, which took effect in June 1961. The number has
69 since grown, making 39 in all. It established Antarctica as
70 a "continent for science and peace," and temporarily sets
71 aside all claims of sovereignty for as long as the Treaty re-
72 mains in effect.
73   The rules of the Treaty meant that as tourists to Antarc-
74 tica, passengers on our cruise ship needed neither pass-
75 ports nor visas. Except for a handful of sites of special
76 scientific interest, specially protected areas, and specially
77 managed areas, there was nothing to restrict us from wan-
78 dering anywhere we wanted.
79   Primarily because of its scientific and ecological impor-
80 tance, many scientists feel that Antarctica should be dedi-
81 cated to research only. They feel that tourists should not
82 be permitted to come. However, recent events have shown
83 that the greatest future threat to Antarctica may not be
84 tourism or scientific stations, but the worldwide thirst for
85 oil and minerals. "The reason the Antarctic Treaty was ne-
86 gotiated and went through so quickly," geologist John
87 Splettstoesser explains, "is that at the time, relatively few
88 minerals were known to exist there."
89   By the early 1970s, however, there were some indica-
90 tions that there might be gas and oil in Antarctica. The
91 treaty countries decided that no commercial companies
92 would be permitted to explore for resources. The Madrid
93 Protocol bans all exploration or commercial exploitation of
94 natural resources on the continent for the next 50 years.
95   Like the Antarctic Treaty itself, the Madrid Protocol is
96 binding only on the 39 Treaty countries. There's nothing to
97 stop non-Treaty countries from establishing commercial
98 bases anywhere on the continent and doing whatever they
99 please.
100   Where do we go from here? So far, no non-Treaty nation
101 has expressed a serious interest in setting up for business
102 in Antarctica. So far, none of the countries claiming sover-
103 eignty has moved to formally annex Antarctic territory.

104   So whose continent is Antarctica, anyway? Vice Presi-
105 dent Albert Gore best expresses the feelings of those of us
106 who have fallen in love with this strange and spectacular
107 land: "I think that it should be held in trust as a global eco-
108 logical reserve for all the people of the world, not just in
109 this generation, but later generations to come as well."

• A. Fact-Finding Exercise

Read the passage once. Then read the following statements. Scan the article quickly to find out if each statement is true (T) or false (F). If a statement is false, change it so that it is true.

_____ T _____ F   1. Most people agree that Antarctica should be
                           used for research.

_____ T _____ F   2. Antarctica is the coldest place on earth.

_____ T _____ F   3. Most of Antarctica is ice-free.

_____ T _____ F 4. Antarctica is a useless continent.

_____ T _____ F 5. Important information about the past may be buried under the Antarctic ice.

_____ T _____ F 6. Thirty-nine countries have agreed to the Antarctic Treaty.

_____ T _____ F 7. Most tourists feel that Antarctica should be dedicated to scientific research only.

_____ T _____ F 8. The Madrid Protocol allows countries to explore Antarctica for natural resources.

• B. Reading Analysis

Read each question carefully. Circle the number or letter of the correct answer, or write your answer in the space provided.

1. Read lines 1–3. What is the ***World Discoverer***?

   _____

2. In line 1, who does **our** refer to?

   _____

3. Read lines 3–5. What is as large as France?
   a. the *World Discoverer*
   b. the Ross Ice Shelf
   c. Antarctica

4. a. In line 7, what follows the colon (:)?
      1. additional information
      2. an example
      3. an explanation
   b. In line 7, what is an **irresistible attraction**?

      _____

      _____

5. Read lines 6–8: "We had been lured by an irresistible attraction: the chance to visit the most remote place on Earth." What does **lure** mean?
   a. invite
   b. visit
   c. attract

6. In lines 8 and 9, what is the coldest place on Earth?

   _____

7. Read lines 12–18. In line 16, who does **others** refer to?
   a. tourists
   b. scientists
   c. environmentalists
   d. oil and mineral seekers

8. In lines 28–29, what does **a mere 2.4 percent** mean?
   a. only 2.4 percent
   b. exactly 2.4 percent
   c. approximately 2.4 percent

9. Read lines 43–45. Which one of the following examples represents a **food chain**?
   a. orange tree → oranges → people
   b. insects → birds → cats
   c. farmer → supermarket → people

10. Read lines 60 and 61. What is **IGY**?

   _____

11. a. Read lines 59–62. When was Antarctica thought of as a useless continent?
      1. before IGY
      2. after IGY
    b. When did scientists begin the first serious study of Antarctica?
      1. before 1957
      2. 1957–1958
      3. after 1958

12. Read lines 66–67. "As IGY wound down, the question of who owns Antarctica came to a head." What does **came to a head** mean?
    a. started a big argument
    b. grew to a large size
    c. became very important

13. In line 72, what does **sovereignty** mean?
    a. ownership
    b. boundaries
    c. continent

14. In line 76, what is **a handful**?
    a. a small number
    b. a large number

15. Read lines 76–79. Which word is a synonym for **sites**?

   _____

16. In lines 86–89, when does **at the time** refer to?

   _____

17. In line 98, what are **non-Treaty countries**?

   _____

18. a. In lines 101 and 103, what does **so far** mean?
     1. in the future
     2. up to now
     3. never
    b. Why do the authors write **so far** twice in the same paragraph?
     1. for repetition
     2. for contrast
     3. for emphasis

19. Read the last paragraph, especially lines 108–110. Who thinks this way about Antarctica?
    a. only Albert Gore
    b. the authors
    c. everyone who loves Antarctica

• C. Word Forms

Part 1

In English, many verbs become nouns by adding the suffix -ment, for example, *improve* (v.), *improvement* (n.).
    Complete each sentence with the correct form of the words on the left. **Use the correct tense of the verbs, in either the affirmative or the negative form. Use the singular or plural form of the nouns.**

employ (v.)
employment (n.)

1. a. In the past, many companies had very unfair _____ practices.
   b. For example, they _____ anyone they were prejudiced against, and they often made people work six or even seven days a week.

establish (v.)
establishment (n.)

2. a. The government recently _____ an agency to investigate reports of environmental pollution.
   b. Many private environmental groups praised the government for its timely _____ of this agency.

govern (v.)
government (n.)

3. a. I'm going to vote for Joan Harrington for mayor because I think that our city _____ needs a change.

    b. I really believe that Joan _____ the city much better than the present mayor has been doing.

manage (v.)
management (n.)

4. a. Bill and Carla _____ the new Computer Industries company together, beginning next year.

    b. The Board of Directors believes that the new _____ will help the company improve its productivity over the next five years.

equip (v.)
equipment (n.)

5. a. The manager of Fielder's Choice always _____ the high school baseball team.

    b. He provides the team with all the basic _____ it needs in return for having his shop's name on the team's uniforms.

Part 2

In English, many verbs become nouns by adding the suffix *-ion* or *-tion*, for example, *suggest* (v.), *suggestion* (n.).

Complete each sentence with the correct form of the words on the left. **Use the correct tense of the verbs, in either the affirmative or the negative form. Use the singular or plural form of the nouns.**

reflect (v.)
reflection (n.)

1. a. The baby saw her _____ in the mirror and smiled.

    b. She didn't understand that the mirror actually _____ her own image, not another child's.

reduce (v.)
reduction (n.)

2. a. Neil _____ the amount of food he eats because he has gone on a diet.

    b. He is working on a weight _____ of ten to fifteen pounds in a month.

deplete (v.)
depletion (n.)

3. a. We _____ the world's supply of oil and natural gas at a steady rate.

   b. In order to reduce the rate of _____ of these natural resources, we need to resort to alternate sources of energy.

exploit (v.)
exploitation (n.)

4. a. If we _____ our natural resources wisely, and take care to protect the environment, we will have a supply of oil and gas for a long time.

   b. However, it is very easy for unwise _____ to leave the Earth both polluted and without resources.

negotiate (v.)
negotiation (n.)

5. a. The two computer firms entered into serious _____ in order to merge their companies into one.

   b. They not only _____ acceptable terms, but also decided where to relocate the newly formed company.

• D. Dictionary Skills

Choose the appropriate definition for each word. Then write the number and the synonym or meaning in the space provided. Remember that you may need to change the wording of the definition in order to have a grammatically correct sentence.

1. **remote** *adj*   **1** separated by an interval or space greater than usual **2** far removed in space, time, or relation: DIVERGENT **3** out-of-the-way, secluded **4** acting, acted on, or controlled indirectly or from a distance **5** small in degree: SLIGHT

   Think of a place as (____) _____ as the far side of the moon.

2. **contend** *v*   **1** to strive or vie in contest or rivalry or against difficulties: STRUGGLE **2** to strive in debate: ARGUE **3** maintain, assert **4** to struggle for: CONTEST

   Some people (____) _____ that preserving Antarctica as a kind of world park will deprive the rest of the world of oil and mineral reserves.

3. **dismiss** *v*   **1** to permit or cause to leave   **2** to remove from position or service: DISCHARGE   **3 a** to bar from attention or serious consideration   **b** to put out of judicial consideration

Until scientists began the first serious study of Antarctica in 1957, most people (_____)_____ the continent. They considered it a vast, useless place.

4. **annex** *v*   **1** to attach as a quality, consequence, or condition   **2** to add to something earlier, larger, or more important   **3** to incorporate (a country or other territory) within the domain of a state   **4** to obtain or take for oneself

So far, none of the countries claiming sovereignty over Antarctica has moved to formally (_____)_____ it _____.

• E. Information Organization

Read the article a second time. Underline what you think are the main ideas. Then scan the article and complete the following outline, using the sentences that you have underlined to help you. You will use this outline later to answer specific questions about the article.

I. People with Conflicting Interests in Antarctica

    A.
       reason:
    B. tourists
       reason: They prize the chance to visit Earth's last frontier
    C.
       reason:
    D.
       reason:

II. The Madrid Protocol

    A. date:
    B. original number of participating nations:
    C. purpose:

III.

    A.
    B.
    C. Winds blow at more than 200 mph

    D.
    E. There are no villages, towns, or plants

IV. Antarctica Is Vital to Life on Earth

    A.
    B.
    C.
    D.

V. The Antarctic Treaty's Purpose

    A.
    B.
    C.

• F. Information Organization Quiz and Summary

Read each question carefully. Use your notes to answer the questions. Do not refer back to the text. Write your answers in the space provided under each question. When you are finished, write a brief summary of the article.

1. Why are there conflicting interests regarding Antarctica?

    _____

    _____

2. What is the Madrid Protocol?

    _____

    _____

3. Describe the continent of Antarctica.

    _____

    _____

4. Is Antarctica necessary to life on Earth? Why, or why not?

    _____

    _____

5. What is the purpose of the Antarctic Treaty?

    _____

    _____

Summary

_____

_____

_____

_____

• G. Critical Thinking Strategies

Read each question carefully. Write your response in the space provided. Remember that there is no one correct answer. Your response depends on what **you** think.

1. Read lines 30–33. What do you think would happen if sea levels rose 200 feet?

   _____

   _____

   _____

   _____

2. Read lines 54–58. What do you think are some other reasons that it may be important to study ancient climates?

   _____

   _____

   _____

   _____

3. Read lines 86–89. When the Antarctic Treaty was signed in 1961, very little was known about the continent's natural resources. According to John Splettstoesser, what is the relationship between the quick signing of the treaty and the lack of information about the resources?

   _____

   _____

   _____

   _____

• H. Follow-up Discussion and Activities

1. Scientists, tourists, environmentalists, and oil and mineral seekers all have different opinions about what to do with Antarctica. Choose one of these four groups, and imagine that you are a member. Working with a partner or in a small group, make a list of reasons why Antarctica is important to your particular group. Compare your list with your classmates' lists. Then as a class decide which group has the strongest reasons to support its point of view.

2. Form a panel of experts. Write a set of guidelines for the protection and use of Antarctica by all the interested countries of the world. You want to be fair to all the interested countries. You also want to try to satisfy the four groups previously mentioned: scientists, environmentalists, tourists, and oil and mineral seekers.

3. The authors ask who Antarctica belongs to. Whose continent *is* Antarctica? Do you think it should belong to one country, many countries, or to no one? Write a composition explaining your opinion.

4. Reread the fifth paragraph. In this paragraph, the authors describe Antarctica by comparing it with other places and by giving facts about it. The authors are trying to convey an image and a feeling about this unusual continent. Imagine that you keep a journal and that you are visiting Antarctica. Write a journal entry in which you describe what you see and how being in Antarctica makes you feel. Do you have feelings similar to those of the first explorers?

5. In the third paragraph, the authors say that tourists consider Antarctica to be Earth's last frontier. However, other people do not agree with this statement. They believe that there are other places on Earth that have not yet been fully explored and that are still exciting, challenging places to go to. Alone, or with a partner, decide what other such places exist on Earth and examine why people would be very interested in going there.

• Library Resource Mastery

Chapter 3 gave examples of title and author cards. Very often, however, people who go to the library to look for a book do not have an author or a book title in mind. In this case, they need to look for a book under the subject they are interested in.

To locate a book on people who have explored Antarctica, for example, you might want to look under *SOUTH POLE, SCIENTIFIC EXPEDI-TIONS,* or *ANTARCTIC REGIONS.* If you want to be more specific, you could look under *ANTARCTIC REGIONS: Discovery and Exploration,* or *SCIENTIFIC EXPEDITIONS—ANTARCTIC REGIONS.* If you are not sure, ask the librarian to assist you.

• Library Assignment

Antarctica has always fascinated people. Many people have tried to explore it and to reach the South Pole, for example, Robert Falcon Scott and Roald Amundsen, and, most recently, Will Steger and five others. Some of the Antarctic explorers died in their attempts.

Go to the library and find a book on Antarctica. Read about the explorers who went there. Read the entries they wrote in their diaries. Prepare an oral report for your class on one of these explorers or group of explorers.

A Messenger From the Past

by James Shreeve
Discover

• **Prereading Preparation**

1. Do you think it's important to learn about humans of the past? Why, or why not?
2. What are some ways we can learn about humans of the past?
3. Read the title of this article and look at the picture on the left. Who is the messenger from the past? What message, or information, can he give us today?

1　　His people said good-bye and watched him walk off to-
2　ward the mountains. They had little reason to fear for his
3　safety: the man was well dressed in insulated clothing and
4　equipped with tools needed to survive the Alpine climate.
5　However, as weeks passed without his return, they must
6　have grown worried, then anxious, and finally resigned.
7　After many years everyone who knew him had died, and
8　not even a memory of the man remained.
9　　Then, on an improbably distant day, he came down
10　from the mountain. Things had changed a bit: it wasn't the
11　Bronze Age anymore, and he was a celebrity.
12　　When a melting glacier released its hold on a 4,000-
13　year-old corpse in September, it was quite rightly called
14　one of the most important archeological finds of the cen-
15　tury. Discovered by a German couple hiking at 10,500 feet
16　in the Italian Tyrol near the Austrian border, the partially
17　freeze-dried body still wore remnants of leather garments
18　and boots that had been stuffed with straw for insulation.
19　The hikers alerted scientists from the University of
20　Innsbruck in Austria, whose more complete examination
21　revealed that the man was tattooed on his back and behind

22 his knee. At his side was a bronze ax of a type typical in
23 southern central Europe around 2000 B.C. On his expedi-
24 tion—perhaps to hunt or to search for metal ore—he had
25 also carried an all-purpose stone knife, a wooden back-
26 pack, a bow and a quiver, a small bag containing a flint
27 lighter and kindling, and an arrow repair kit in a leather
28 pouch.

29   Such everyday gear gives an unprecedented perspec-
30 tive on life in early Bronze Age Europe. "The most exciting
31 thing is that we genuinely appear to be looking at a man
32 who had some kind of accident in the course of a perfectly
33 ordinary trip," says archeologist Ian Kinnes of the British
34 Museum. "These are not artifacts placed in a grave, but the
35 fellow's own possessions."

36   Unlike the Egyptians and Mesopotamians of the time,
37 who had more advanced civilizations with cities and cen-
38 tral authority, the Ice Man and his countrymen lived in a
39 society built around small, stable villages. He probably
40 spoke in a tongue ancestral to current European languages.
41 Furthermore, though he was a member of a farming cul-
42 ture, he may well have been hunting when he died, to add
43 meat to his family's diet. X-rays of the quiver showed that
44 it contained 14 arrows. While his backpack was empty,
45 careful exploration of the trench where he died revealed
46 remnants of animal skin and bones at the same spot where
47 the pack lay. There was also the remainder of a pile of ber-
48 ries. Clearly the man didn't starve to death.

49   So why did the Ice Man die? The trench provided him
50 with shelter from the elements, and he also had a braided
51 mat of grass to keep him warm. If injury or illness caused
52 the Ice Man's death, an autopsy on the 4,000-year-old vic-
53 tim could turn up some clues. The circumstances of his
54 death may have preserved such evidence, as well as other
55 details of his life. Freeze-dried by the frigid climate, his in-
56 ner organs and other soft tissues are much better pre-
57 served than those of dried-up Egyptian mummies or the
58 waterlogged Scandinavian "Bog Men" found in recent years.

59   One concern, voiced by archeologist Colin Renfrew of
60 Cambridge University, is that the hot TV lights that greeted
61 the hunter's return to civilization may have damaged these
62 fragile tissues, jeopardizing a chance to recover additional
63 precious genetic information from his chromosomes. If
64 not, Renfrew says, "it may be possible to get very long DNA
65 sequences out of this material. This is far and away the
66 most exciting aspect of the discovery."

67   For the time being, all biological research has literally
68 been put on ice at the University of Innsbruck while an in-
69 ternational team of experts, led by researcher Konrad
70 Spindler, puzzles out a way to thaw the body without de-
71 stroying it. As sensational as it sounds, it remains to be
72 seen how useful 4,000-year-old human DNA will really be.
73 "The problem is that we are dealing with a single indi-
74 vidual," says evolutionary biologist Robert Sokal of the
75 State University of New York at Stony Brook. "In order to
76 make statements about the population that existed at the
77 time, we need more specimens."
78   The wish for more messengers from the past may yet
79 come true. Five more bodies of mountain climbers, all of
80 whom died within the past 50 years, have emerged from
81 melting Austrian mountain ice this summer. The Ice Man's
82 return from the Tyrol has demonstrated that the local cli-
83 mate is warmer now than it has been for 4,000 years.
84 People are beginning to wonder—and plan for—what the
85 melting ice may reveal next.
86   "No one ever thought this could happen," says Christo-
87 pher Stringer, an anthropologist at the Natural History Mu-
88 seum in London. "The fact that it has occurred once means
89 that people will now be looking for it again."

• A. Fact-Finding Exercise

Read the passage once. Then read the following statements. Scan the article quickly to find out if each statement is true (T) or false (F). If a statement is false, change it so that it is true.

_____ T _____ F   1. The Ice Man lived 4,000 years ago.

_____ T _____ F   2. The Ice Man was discovered in Europe by scientists.

_____ T _____ F   3. Scientists aren't sure how the Ice Man died.

_____ T _____ F   4. The Ice Man's body had been frozen for 4,000 years.

_____ T _____ F   5. Scientists have examined the Ice Man to get genetic information.

_____ T _____ F   6. More bodies of mountain climbers who died 4,000 years ago were discovered.

• B. Reading Analysis

Read each question carefully. Circle the number or letter of the correct answer, or write your answer in the space provided.

1. Read lines 9 and 10. This statement means
   a. the Ice Man walked down from the mountain.
   b. the Ice Man woke up in the mountain.
   c. the Ice Man's body was brought down from the mountain.

2. In lines 12 and 13, what does the **4,000-year-old corpse** refer to?

   _____

3. Read lines 19–22. **Whose** refers to
   a. the Ice Man.
   b. the scientists.
   c. the hikers.

4. Read lines 19–30.
   a. What are some examples of the Ice Man's **everyday gear**?

   _____

   _____

   b. **Gear** means
      1. clothes.
      2. equipment.
      3. weapons.

5. Read lines 39 and 40. In this sentence, what does **tongue** refer to?
   a. the Ice Man's mouth
   b. the Ice Man's accent
   c. the Ice Man's language

6. In line 41, what follows **furthermore**?
   a. an example
   b. a theory
   c. additional information

7. Read line 48. What does **clearly** mean?
   a. unfortunately
   b. obviously
   c. possibly

8. Read lines 51–55.
   a. In line 54, what does **evidence** mean?
      1. proof of how the Ice Man died
      2. clues to how the Ice Man died
      3. theories describing how the Ice Man may have died
   b. In line 54, what does **as well as** mean?
      1. better than
      2. as good as
      3. in addition to

9. Read lines 53–62. What are the Ice Man's **inner organs and other soft tissues**?
   a. parts of his body
   b. objects he had with him
   c. the food remaining in his stomach

10. In line 65, **far and away** indicates
    a. distance.
    b. importance.
    c. excitement.

11. Read lines 67–71.
    a. **For the time being** means
       1. for a long time.
       2. for now.
       3. for a human being.
    b. **Thaw** means
       1. melt, as ice becomes water.
       2. bring back to life.
       3. bring back to normal temperature.

12. In line 78, **yet** means
    a. still.
    b. but.
    c. not.

13. Read lines 88 and 89. What does **it** refer to?

_____

_____

• C. Word Forms

Part 1

In English, many verbs become nouns by adding the suffix *-ion* or *-tion*, for example, *stimulate* (v.), *stimulation* (n.).
    Complete each sentence with the correct form of the words on the left. **Use the correct tense of the verbs, in either the affirmative or the negative form. Use the singular or plural form of the nouns.**

insulate (v.)   1. a. Nicholas put fiberglass between the
insulation (n.)   outside and inside walls of his house in or-
                           der to provide good _____.
                      b. He also _____ the roof with fiber-
                           glass; consequently, he saved money on
                           his heating bills last winter.

demonstrate (v.)   2. a. Many power companies provide clear
demonstration (n.)   and simple _____ to their customers
                           on how to save on utility and heating bills.
                      b. The companies _____ how to
                           insulate a home and what types of light
                           bulbs and air conditioners save electricity.

explore (v.)

exploration (n.)

3. a. When we go on vacation, we _____ the Adirondack Mountains on foot.

    b. As part of our extensive _____, we are going to investigate some underground caverns, too.

preserve (v.)

preservation (n.)

4. a. Many people are interested in the permanent _____ of undeveloped land in Alaska.

    b. If we _____ this land now, it will be exploited by major oil companies.

destroy (v.)

destruction (n.)

5. a. Eddie was accused of willful _____ of property when he threw a rock through his neighbor's window.

    b. He apparently _____ the window after he had an argument with his neighbor.

Part 2

In English, the noun and verb forms of some words are the same, for example, *promise* (v.), *promise* (n.).

Complete each sentence with the correct form of the words on the left. **Use the correct tense of the verbs, in either the affirmative or the negative form. Use the singular or plural form of the nouns. In addition, indicate whether you are using the verb (v.) or the noun (n.) form of the word.**

alert

1. a. The police department put the town on _____ after a criminal escaped from
        (v., n.)
        the nearby prison.

    b. After they _____ everyone, they
        (v., n.)
        began a systematic search of the area in order to find the escaped convict.

repair

2. a. I called in a plumber to fix the leak under

   my kitchen sink, but he _____ the
   (v., n.)
   leak properly, and water continued to drip.

   b. I decided to buy a book on plumbing and I

   made the _____ myself.
   (v., n.)

return

3. a. Perry is going to the store now, but he

   _____ by 6 o'clock. He is going
   (v., n.)
   to take back a shirt that doesn't fit.

   b. The store accepts both _____ and
   (v., n.)
   exchanges. Perry wants an exchange; he

   wants the same shirt, but in the correct size.

release

4. a. Film companies in the United States usually

   _____ about 20 major films a year.
   (v., n.)

   b. They always advertise their new _____
   (v., n.)
   on television, radio, and in magazines.

damage

5. a. The flood caused considerable property

   _____ to homes near the river.
   (v., n.)

   b. The muddy water ruined many people's

   homes, but, fortunately, it _____ any
   (v., n.)
   major buildings or contaminate the water

   supply.

• D. Dictionary Skills

Choose the appropriate definition for each word. Then write the number and the synonym or meaning in the space provided. Remember that you may need to change the wording of the definition in order to have a grammatically correct sentence.

1. **remnant** *n*   **1 a** a usually small part, member, or trace remaining **b** a small surviving group   **2** an unsold or unused end of piece goods

   The Ice Man's body still wore (___)_____ of leather garments

   and boots that had been stuffed with straw for insulation.

2. **ordinary** *adj*   **1** of a kind to be expected in the normal order of events: ROUTINE, USUAL   **2** having or constituting immediate or original jurisdiction   **3 a** of common quality, rank or ability   **b** deficient in quality: POOR, INFERIOR

   The Ice Man had some kind of accident in the course of a perfectly

   (___)_____ trip.

3. **stable** *adj*   **1 a** firmly established: FIXED, STEADFAST   **b** not changing or fluctuating: UNVARYING   **c** PERMANENT, ENDURING   **2 a** steady in purpose: firm in resolution **b** not subject to insecurity or emotional illness: SANE, RATIONAL   **3** not readily altering in chemical makeup or physical state

   The Ice Man and his countrymen lived in a society built around small,

   (___)_____villages.

4. **element** *n*   **1 a** one of the four substances air, water, fire, and earth formerly believed to compose the physical universe   **b** *pl*: weather conditions caused by activities of the elements; *esp*: violent or severe weather **2 a** a basic member of a mathematical or logical class or set   **b** one of the necessary data or values on which calculations or conclusions are based

   The trench provided the Ice Man with shelter from the (___)_____,

   and he also had a braided mat of grass to keep him warm.

• E. Information Organization

Read the article a second time. Underline what you think are the main ideas. Then scan the article and complete the following flowchart, using the sentences that you have underlined to help you. For each possible cause of death, indicate *yes*, *no*, or *maybe*, based on your reasoning from the information in the text. You will use this flowchart later to answer specific questions about the article.

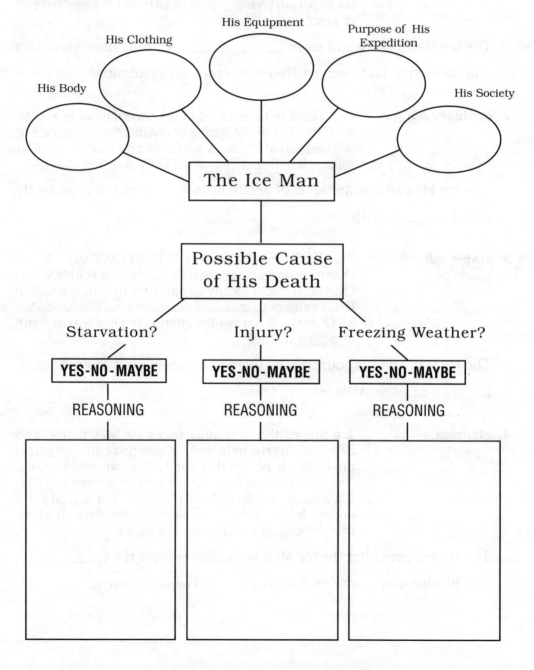

• F. Information Organization Quiz and Summary

Read each question carefully. Use your notes to answer the questions. Do not refer back to the text. Write your answers in the space provided under each question. When you are finished, write a brief summary of the article.

1. a. What was the Ice Man wearing when he was found?

_____

   b. What marks did the Ice Man have on his body?

_____

_____

2. a. What did the Ice Man have with him?

_____

_____

   b. What might he have been doing before he died?

_____

_____

3. Describe the society that the Ice Man lived in.

_____

_____

4. What are some clues as to how the Ice Man died?

_____

_____

Summary

_____

_____

_____

_____

_____

• G. Critical Thinking Strategies

Read each question carefully. Write your response in the space provided. Remember that there is no one correct answer. Your response depends on what **you** think.

1. In the first paragraph of the article, the author gives a personalized description of what happened to the Ice Man 4,000 years ago and how his friends and family may have felt about his loss. What do you think the tone or feeling of this paragraph is? How is the tone and style different from the rest of the article? Why do you think the author started the article in this way?

    _____

    _____

    _____

    _____

2. In the third paragraph, James Shreeve writes that the discovery of the Ice Man "was quite rightly called one of the most important archeological finds of the century." What do you think Shreeve's opinion of this discovery is? Why do you think so?

    _____

    _____

    _____

3. In describing the equipment that the Ice Man had with him, Ian Kinnes points out that they "are not artifacts placed in a grave, but the fellow's own possessions." Why do you think this is so important? Why might objects in a grave be different from what a man normally carries with him for a day or a week?

    _____

    _____

    _____

    _____

4. In lines 36–43, the author describes the society that the Ice Man lived in and compares it with the civilizations of the Egyptians and Mesopotamians of the same time period. How do you think James Shreeve knows what the Ice Man's society was like? How does he know what Egyptian and Mesopotamian society was like at that time?

_____

_____

_____

_____

5. The article informs us that "the Ice Man's return from the Tyrol has demonstrated that the local climate is warmer now than it has been for 4,000 years." What inferences can we make from this statement? What do you think may happen in the future as a result of a warmer climate?

_____

_____

_____

_____

• H. Follow-up Discussion and Activities

1. Imagine that you were the Ice Man 4,000 years ago. Write a journal/diary of your last week alive. Describe what you did, where you went, the people you met, and your last hours alive.

2. According to Robert Sokal, an evolutionary biologist at the State University of New York at Stony Brook, we need to find many examples of preserved people from 4,000 years ago in order to "make statements about the population that existed at the time." What information do you think we can learn from such discoveries? How might this information be useful to us in the twentieth century?

3. If you could ask the Ice Man questions about himself and his time, what would you ask? Work with a partner and make a list of questions. Compare your list with your classmates' lists.

• Library Resource Mastery

Periodicals

1. What are periodicals?

_____

_____

2. Give the names of two or three popular periodicals.

_____

The library does not use the same system for books as it does to keep track of all the periodicals it contains. Libraries use the *Reader's Guide to Periodical Literature*, which is updated monthly. At the beginning of the *Reader's Guide* there is a list of the periodicals that are indexed in the *Guide*. The articles published in each periodical are organized in the *Guide* by topic.

Below is a sample from the *Reader's Guide to Periodical Literature.*

MAN, PREHISTORIC
> *See also*
> Archeology

Digging beneath the Silk Road. J.W. Olsen. il maps *Natural History* 101:30-9 S '92

Iceman [Stone Age mummy found in the Alps; cover story] L. Jaroff. il map *Time* 140:62-6 O 26 '92

The long-lost hunter [frozen Stone Age corpse found in Austrian glacier] S. Harrigan. il *Audubon* 94:92-6 S/O '92

Mitochondrial Eve: wounded, but not dead yet. A. Gibbons. il. *Science* 257:873-5 Ag 14 '92

The world in 3300 B.C. [cover story] M. D. Lemonick. il map *Time* 140:66-9 O 26 '92

1. What topic is the Ice Man listed under?

_____

2. a. Which magazines published articles on the Ice Man?

_____

b. What issues of these magazines are these articles in? Give the month, day, and year for each.

1. _____

2. _____

c. Which pages in each magazine are these articles on?

1. _____

2. _____

Find out if your school or local library carries the magazines that appear in the *Reader's Guide* sample. Each library prints a listing of the periodicals it subscribes to. It may be called *Serials Available in the Library* or have a similar name. The listing also indicates the call number for each periodical and how it is kept in the library, e.g., bound in hard cover or on microfilm. Ask the librarian for help.

3. What is the name of the reference "book" that lists the periodicals that the library carries?

_____

4. Where is this book located in your school or local library?

_____

• Library Assignment

The article titled "Messenger from the Past" was written before scientists published the results of their study on the Ice Man and his possessions. More recent articles will have more detailed information. They may also contain some revised information on the Ice Man, because some of the guesses that scientists made initially may have been incorrect.

1. Go to the library.
   a. Locate one of the articles listed in the *Reader's Guide* example or another recent article on the Ice Man.
   b. Photocopy the article. Read it and bring it to class.
   c. In small groups, refer to the following table. With the up-to-date information your group now has, check the information from the article "Messenger from the Past." If the information is correct, leave it. If the information has been shown to be incorrect, change it.

	Original Information (Source): "Messenger from the Past"- Discover, Jan. 1992	Revised Information (Source):
When the Ice Man lived	4,000 years ago	
The Age the Ice Man lived in	the Bronze Age	
The Ice Man's age at death	(unknown)	
The Ice Man's physical condition	uninjured	
The marks on the Ice Man's body	tattoos on his back and behind his knee	
The Ice Man's equipment	1. clothes made of leather 2. a bronze ax 3. a bow, arrows, and a quiver	

d. Compare your table with your classmates' tables. Which article(s) had the most detailed and correct information?

2. According to this article, the Ice Man lived 4,000 years ago in the Bronze Age. His society was very different from the civilizations of Egypt and Mesopotamia of the same time period. Select an area of the world, perhaps your own. Refer to "The World in 3300 B.C.," (the article in the *Reader's Guide* listing), a history book or an encyclopedia, or your own knowledge. Write a description of what life was like 5,000 years ago for the people in the society you have chosen. Discuss how their lives and the lives of Ice Man and his people were similar and how they were different.

AGES OF MANKIND

B.C.	
	"Iron Age"
500	
1000	Chalcolithic "Bronze Age"
2000	
3000	Neolithic "New Stone Age"
4000	
5000	
6000	Mesolithic "Middle Stone Age"
7000	
8000	
9000	Paleolithic "Old Stone Age"
10000	

C·H·A·P·T·E·R 12

Is Time Travel Possible?

by Mark Davidson

USA Today

• Prereading Preparation

1. What is **time travel**?
2. Do you think time travel may be possible? Why, or why not?
3. Do you think scientists should try to find a way to travel to the past? To the future? Why, or why not?
4. Would you like to travel to the past? If you would, where would you go?
5. Would you like to travel to the future? If you would, where would you go? Using the chart below, take a survey of your classmates. Compare your classmates' responses.

STUDENT'S NAME	Would you like to travel to the past? Yes/No	Where would you like to go?	Would you like to travel to the future? Yes/No	Where would you like to go?

1   Contrary to the old warning that time waits for no one,
2 time slows down when you are on the move. It also slows
3 down more as you move faster, which means astronauts
4 someday may survive so long in space that they would re-
5 turn to an Earth of the distant future. If you could move at
6 the speed of light, 186,282 miles a second, your time
7 would stand still. If you could move faster than light, your
8 time would move backward.

9   Although no form of matter yet discovered moves as
10 fast or faster than light, scientific experiments have con-
11 firmed that accelerated motion causes a voyager's, or
12 traveler's, time to be stretched. Albert Einstein predicted
13 this in 1905, when he introduced the concept of relative
14 time as part of his Special Theory of Relativity. A search is
15 now under way to confirm the suspected existence of par-
16 ticles of matter that move faster than light and therefore
17 possibly might serve as our passports to the past.

18   An obsession with time—saving, gaining, wasting, los-
19 ing, and mastering it—seems to have been part of human-
20 ity for as long as humans have existed. Humanity also has
21 been obsessed with trying to capture the *meaning* of time.
22 Einstein used a definition of time, for experimental pur-
23 poses, as that which is measured by a clock. Thus, time
24 and time's relativity are measurable by any sundial, hour-
25 glass, metronome, alarm clock, or an atomic clock that can
26 measure a billionth of a second.

27   Scientists have demonstrated that an ordinary airplane
28 flight is like a brief visit to the Fountain of Youth. In 1972,
29 for example, scientists who took four atomic clocks on an
30 airplane trip around the world discovered that the moving
31 clocks moved slightly slower than atomic clocks which had
32 remained on the ground. If you fly around the world, pref-
33 erably going eastward to gain the advantage of the added
34 motion of the Earth's rotation, the atomic clocks show that
35 you'll return younger than you would have been if you had
36 stayed home. Frankly, you'll be younger by only 40 bil-
37 lionths of a second. Even such an infinitesimal saving of
38 time proves that time can be stretched. Moreover, atomic
39 clocks have demonstrated that the stretching of time in-
40 creases with speed.

41   Here is an example of what you can expect if tomor-
42 row's space-flight technology enables you to move at ultra-

---

[1]This hypothetical situation is known as the Twin Paradox.

43 high speeds. Imagine you're an astronaut with a twin who
44 stays home.[1] If you travel back and forth to the nearest star
45 at about half the speed of light, you'll be gone for 18 Earth
46 years. When you return, your twin will be 18 years older,
47 but you'll have aged only 16 years. Your body will be two
48 years younger than your twin's because time aboard the
49 flying spaceship will have moved more slowly than time
50 on Earth. You will have aged normally, but you have been
51 in a slower time zone. If your spaceship moves at about
52 90% of lightspeed, you'll age only 50% as much as your
53 twin. If you whiz along at 99.86% of lightspeed, you'll age
54 only five percent as much. These examples of time-stretch-
55 ing, of course, cannot be tested with any existing space-
56 craft. They are based on mathematical projections of
57 relativity science.
58   Speed is not the only factor that slows time; so does
59 gravity. Einstein determined in his General Theory of Rela-
60 tivity that the force of an object's gravity "curves" the
61 space in the object's gravitational field. When gravity
62 curves space, Einstein reasoned, gravity also must curve
63 time, because space and time are linked.
64   Numerous atomic clock experiments have confirmed
65 Einstein's calculation that, the closer you are to the Earth's
66 center of gravity, which is the Earth's core, the slower you
67 will age. In one of these experiments, an atomic clock was
68 taken from the National Bureau of Standards in Washing-
69 ton, D.C., near sea level, and moved to mile-high Denver.
70 The results demonstrated that people in Denver age more
71 rapidly by a tiny amount than people in Washington.
72   If you would like gravity's space-time warp to extend
73 your life, get a home at the beach and a job as a deep-sea
74 diver. Avoid living in the mountains or working in a sky-
75 scraper. That advice, like the advice about flying around
76 the world, will enable you to slow your aging by only a few
77 billionths of a second. Nevertheless, those tiny fractions of
78 a second add up to more proof that time-stretching is a re-
79 ality.

80 **Time Reversal**
81   According to scientific skeptics, time reversal—travel
82 to the past—for humans would mean an unthinkable rever-
83 sal of cause and effect. This reversal would permit you to
84 do something in the past that changes the present. The
85 skeptics worry that you even might commit an act that pre-
86 vents your own birth.

87   Some scientists believe we should keep an open mind
88 about time reversal. Open-minders speculate that time-
89 travelers who change the past would be opening doors to
90 *alternative* histories, rather than interfering with history as
91 we know it. For example, if you prevented the assassina-
92 tion of Abraham Lincoln, then a new line of historical de-
93 velopment would be created. The alternative history—the
94 one without Lincoln's assassination—would have a com-
95 pletely separate, ongoing existence. Thus, no change
96 would be made in anybody's existing history. Another pos-
97 sibility is that nature might have an unbreakable law pre-
98 venting time travelers from changing the past.

99 **Journey to the Future**

100   If we did discover a source of energy that would enable
101 us to travel beyond lightspeed, we might have access not
102 only to the past, but also to the future. Suppose you went
103 on a super-lightspeed trek to the Spiral Nebula in the An-
104 dromeda Galaxy. That location is separated from Earth by
105 1,500,000 lightyears, the distance light travels in
106 1,500,000 years. Suppose you make the round trip in just
107 a few moments. If all goes well, you'll return to the Earth
108 3,000,000 years into its future, because that's how much
109 Earth time will have elapsed.

110   Time is an abstraction. In other words, it cannot be
111 seen, touched, smelled, or tasted. It seems to have no ex-
112 istence apart from the events it measures, but something
113 tells us that time is out there, somewhere. "When we pur-
114 sue the meaning of time," according to the time-obsessed
115 English novelist-playwright J. B. Priestly, "we are like a
116 knight on a quest, condemned to wander through innu-
117 merable forests, bewildered and baffled, because the
118 magic beast he is looking for is the horse he is riding."

119   What about our quest for particles that travel faster
120 than light? If we find them, will we be able to control their
121 energy to tour the past? If we return to our past, will we be
122 forced to repeat our mistakes and suffer the same conse-
123 quences? Or will we be able to use our experience to make
124 everything turn out better the second time around?

125   Will we ever be able to take instant trips to the distant
126 future, the way people do in the movies, with a twist of a
127 dial and a "zap!, zap!" of sound effects? One cannot resist
128 the temptation to respond that only time will tell.

• A. Fact-Finding Exercise

Read the passage once. Then read the following statements. Scan the article quickly to find out if each statement is true (T) or false (F). If a statement is false, change it so that it is true.

_____ T _____ F   1. If you could move at the speed of light, your time would move backward.

_____

_____ T _____ F   2. Scientists have discovered a form of matter that moves as fast as light.

_____

_____ T _____ F   3. Scientists have done experiments which show that the stretching of time increases with speed.

_____

_____ T _____ F   4. Both speed and gravity slow time.

_____

_____ T _____ F   5. The closer you are to the Earth's core, the faster you will age.

_____

_____ T _____ F   6. Some people worry that if you could go back in time, you might change the present.

_____

• B. Reading Analysis

Read each question carefully. Circle the number or letter of the correct answer, or write your answer in the space provided.

1. Read lines 5–7.

   a. What is the speed of light?

   _____

   b. In lines 6–7, what does **your time would stand still** mean?
      1. Your time would speed up.
      2. Your time would reverse.
      3. Your time would stop.

2. Read lines 12–13: "Einstein predicted **this** in 1905." What does **this** refer to? In other words, what did Einstein predict?

   _____

   _____

3. Read lines 14–17.

   a. **Under way** means that the search is
      1. being done now.
      2. finished.
      3. under a method.
   b. **Suspected existence** means that
      1. people have found these particles.
      2. people believe these particles exist.
      3. people do not believe these particles exist.
   c. What are our **passports to the past**?

   _____

4. Read lines 27 and 28. In this sentence, scientists mean that an airplane trip might
   a. make you younger.
   b. slow down the aging process.
   c. make you older.

5. Read lines 32–37. **Frankly** means

   a. actually.
   b. on the contrary.
   c. obviously.

6. In lines 36–38, an **infinitesimal** saving of time is

   a. a large amount.
   b. an average amount.
   c. a very small amount.

7. In line 41–42, **tomorrow** refers to

   a. the day after today.
   b. some time in the future.
   c. some time next year.

8. Read lines 43–47.

   a. What is this imaginary situation commonly known as?

   _____

   b. How do you know?

   _____

   c. **Back and forth** means
      1. travel to the nearest star and then return to Earth.
      2. travel to the nearest star two times.
      3. travel back to the nearest star after you've been there.

9. Read lines 51–54. **Whiz** means

   a. age.
   b. change.
   c. move.

10. Read lines 58–63. Why is **"curves"** in quotation marks?

    _____

11. Read lines 88–98. What is this imaginary situation an example of?

    _____

12. Read lines 100–102. What is the purpose of **did**?

    a. to ask a question
    b. to show emphasis
    c. to express the past

13. In line 106, what does **round trip** mean?

    _____

14. Read lines 110–118.

    a. What does **quest** mean?

    _____

    b. How do you know?

    _____

• C. Word Forms

Part 1

In English, some verbs become adjectives by adding the suffix -al, for example, *remove* (v.), *removal* (n.).
    Complete each sentence with the correct form of the words on the left. **Use the correct tense of the verbs, in either the affirmative or the negative form.**

experiment (v.)

experimental (adj.)

1. a. Scientists in the pharmaceutical laboratory are working on a new drug, but it is in the _____ stage. Doctors cannot prescribe it yet.

    b. The scientists _____ successfully with the drug in the laboratory; now they need to test it on human volunteers.

cause (v.)

causal (adj.)

2. a. When researchers try to establish what _____ a given disease, they look for relationships between certain factors and the onset of the disease.

    b. Sometimes it is quite difficult to establish a clear _____ relationship between the disease and a particular factor.

survive (v.)

survival (adj.)

3. a. Mark and Laura were stranded in the mountains in the middle of a severe snowstorm. They needed basic _____ skills in order to stay alive.

    b. They only _____ the bitter cold because they found a small cave, which protected them from the harsh weather until a rescue team found them two days later.

arrive (v.)

arrival (adj.)

4. a. All international passengers must go through the _____ gate into customs before leaving the airport.

    b. Everyone who _____ at the airport must declare what they are bringing into the country.

Part 2

In English, some verbs become nouns by adding the suffix *-ance* or *-ence*, for example, *appear* (v.), *appearance* (n.).

Complete each sentence with the correct form of the words on the left. **Use the correct tense of the verbs, in either the affirmative or the negative form.**

avoid (v.)
avoidance (n.)

1. a. Monica regularly _____ exposure to the sun.
   b. Her careful _____ of the sun is due to persistent skin problems.

resist (v.)
resistance (n.)

2. a. It is a well-known fact that stress lowers the body's _____ to illness.
   b. It is logical, then, that we _____ disease better when we maintain good health and avoid stressful situations.

accept (v.)
acceptance (n.)

3. a. Gloria's English teacher _____ any papers that are more than two days late. This is her policy.
   b. Her professor's _____ of papers also depends on whether the students have followed her guidelines for the format of the paper, such as double spacing.

insist (v.)
insistence (n.)

4. a. Arthur invariably _____ on having dinner at the same time every day.
   b. His odd _____ on the same dinnertime isn't his only habit. He also insists on eating the same breakfast, and going to the same place for vacation every year.

exist (v.)
existence (n.)

5. a. There is a myth about a creature called the Abominable Snowman, which some people believe _____ somewhere in the Himalaya Mountains.
   b. There is also a legend about the _____ of a giant creature called Sasquatch, or Bigfoot, which supposedly lives in the Pacific Northwest.

• D. Dictionary Skills

Choose the appropriate definition for each word. Then write the number and the synonym or meaning in the space provided. Remember that you may need to change the wording of the definition in order to have a grammatically correct sentence.

1. **matter** *n*

  1 a a subject under consideration   **b** a subject of disagreement   **c** the subject or substance of a discourse or writing   **d** problem; difficulty   **2 a** the substance of which a physical object is composed   **b** material substance that occupies space and has weight   **3** something written or printed   **4** a more or less definite amount or quantity

No form of (_____)_____ has yet been discovered that moves as fast or faster than light.

2. **stretch** *v*

  1 to extend (as one's limbs or body) in a reclining position   **2** to reach out: EXTEND   **3** to extend in length   **4 a** to enlarge or distend esp. by force   **b** to extend or expand as if by physical force   **c** strain   **5** to cause to reach or continue (as from one point to another or across a space)

Experiments with atomic clocks show that it is possible to

___(___)_____ time_____.

3. **determine** *v*

  1 a to fix conclusive or authoritatively   **b** to decide by judicial sentence   **c** to settle or decide by choice of alternatives or possibilities   **d** resolve   **2 a** to fix the form, position, or character of beforehand   **b** to bring about as a result: REGULATE   **3 a** to find out or come to a decision about by investigation, reasoning, or calculation   **b** to discover the taxonomic position or the generic and specific names of

Einstein (___)_____ in his General Theory of Relativity that the force of an object's gravity "curves" the space in the object's gravitational field.

4. **speculate** *v*

  1 a to meditate on or ponder a subject: REFLECT   **b** to review something idly or casually and often inconclusively   **2** to assume a business risk in hope of gain

Open-minders (___)_____ that time-travelers who change the past would be opening doors to alternative histories, rather than interfering with known history.

• E. Information Organization

Read the article a second time. Underline what you think are the main ideas. Then scan the article and complete the following table, using the sentences that you have underlined to help you. You will use this table later to answer specific questions about the article. Not all the boxes will be filled in.

	SPEED	GRAVITY
Time speeds up		
Time slows down		
Time stops		
Experimental evidence		
Hypothetical example		

• F. Information Organization Quiz and Summary

Read each question carefully. Use your notes to answer the questions. Do not refer back to the text. Write your answers in the space provided under each question. When you are finished, write a brief summary of the article.

1. How does the speed of light affect time?

   _____

   _____

2. Describe the evidence which shows that time is affected by speed.

   _____

   _____

3. Describe the evidence which shows that time is affected by gravity.

   _____

   _____

4. How would time reversal change cause and effect?

   _____

   _____

Summary

_____

_____

_____

_____

• G. Critical Thinking Strategies

Read each question carefully. Write your response in the space provided. Remember that there is no one correct answer. Your response depends on what **you** think.

1. In line 1, the author refers to a proverb, "Time waits for no one." What do you think this proverb means? Why do you think the author mentioned this proverb with regard to the topic of the reading?

   _____

   _____

   _____

   _____

2. Read lines 54–57. Why do you think time-stretching cannot be tested with any spacecraft we have today?

   _____

   _____

   _____

   _____

3. Read lines 81–86. What do you think **reversal of cause and effect** means? What do you think about this argument against travel to the past?

   _____

   _____

   _____

   _____

4. Read lines 110–118. What do you think is the purpose of this reference to a knight on a quest? In other words, what image do you think the author wants us to visualize? Why?

   _____

   _____

   _____

   _____

• H. Follow-up Discussion and Activities

1. Imagine that you could travel back in time. Choose a person from the past you'd like to meet. Explain why you would like to meet this person.

2. Imagine that you could travel to the past. What is the one historical event you would like to change? Why do you want to change it? How would you change it? What consequences might this change have for the present?

3. Would you like to see the future? Why? What year do you want to visit? Explain.

4. Imagine that time travel is possible. Do you think there should be restrictions on this type of travel? For example, many countries have visa and immigration restrictions. Should there also be re-strictions on time travel? If so, what restrictions do you suggest? Who would be in charge of making these rules and enforcing them?

5. a. Refer to the Time Preference Survey on page 205. Discuss it in class to make sure you understand the questions.
   b. After you have read the questionnaire, go outside your class alone or in pairs. Survey two or three people.
   c. Bring back your data and combine it with the other students' in-formation. Create a bar graph or other chart to compile your data. Divide your responses by past, present, and future. Then divide those responses by gender and/or by age. What do you observe about the responses? Are there any observable patterns by gender or by age? Speculate on the reasons why these groups prefer a particular time.

Time Preference Survey

The purpose of this questionnaire is to collect data regarding people's preferences concerning living in the past, the present, or the future.

Interviewee is _____ Male _____ Female

Interviewee is _____ under 20 _____ 40–50

_____ 20–30 _____ over 50

_____ 30–40

Please answer the following questions.

1. If you could travel to any time, when would it be?

_____ past _____ stay in the present _____ future

2. If you prefer the past, why would you go back?

_____ to live there

_____ to change something, then return to the present

_____ other; please be specific

_____

3. If you prefer the present, why would you stay here?

_____

_____

4. If you prefer the future, why would you go there?

_____

_____

Unit IV Review

• I. Vocabulary Categorization

The words in the vocabulary list below have been taken from the three readings in this unit. Read through the list, and place the words into the four categories indicated. Write in the appropriate heading for the two categories that have been left blank. Remember, some words may belong in more than one category.

advantage	ecology	passenger
agreement	employment	pollution
archeology	equipment	preservation
astronaut	expedition	researcher
attraction	experiment	resources
boundary	exploration	return
cause and effect	government	scientist
civilization	gravity	speculation
cruise	hiker	survival
depletion	management	theory
destruction	negotiation	tourist

Environment _____   **Making Choices** _____

• J. Crossword Puzzle

Across

4. View, opinion
8. Clues, indications
11. Movement
13. We live in the present _____.
14. The _____ is the finish.
16. Severe; strong
19. Searching; looking
20. Huge; extensive
21. Objects; articles
24. Connection
26. Another choice; another possibility
28. The opposite of **lose**
29. I will go _____ it doesn't rain.
30. Observe and guess; reflect

Down

1. Easily damaged; delicate
2. Frozen water
3. Conditions
5. Search
6. A dead body
7. The opposite of **off**
9. Traveler
10. Protect; keep safe
12. Necessary; essential
15. Location; place
17. Connected; related
18. Endanger
22. Extremely cold; frozen
23. To unfreeze; to bring back to normal temperature
25. Forbids; prohibits
27. At a distance

• K. Unit IV Discussion

1. Modern technology has given us insights into the past, the present, and the future. What do you think is the greatest technological advance we have made so far? How will it help us better understand the past, the present, and the future?

2. If time travel to the past were possible today, it would be very easy for us to learn about ancient civilizations. Imagine that time travel to the future is also possible. What do you think would be the biggest advantage to knowing the future? What would be the biggest disadvantage? Explain your answer.

3. Imagine that you could travel 500 years into the future in Antarctica. What do you think you would see there? What country or countries would "own" Antarctica? Why? Explain your answer.

4. People sometimes want to save a "picture" of the time they live in for people in the future to see. They select objects to preserve so that people can look at them at a specific time in the future. A time capsule is a sealed container that people use in order to preserve these objects. You are a member of a committee whose job it is to prepare a time capsule for this year. The time capsule will not be opened until the year 3000. Discuss with the other members of your committee what you would like to put into the time capsule in order to show what this year was like.

Index of Key Words and Phrases

Cloze Quizzes

• Chapter 1: The Paradox of Happiness

Cloze

Read the passage on this page. Fill in the blanks below with one word from the list. Use each word once.

1. _____
2. _____
3. _____
4. _____
5. _____
6. _____
7. _____
8. _____
9. _____
10. _____
11. _____
12. _____
13. _____
14. _____
15. _____
16. _____
17. _____
18. _____
19. _____
20. _____

advice
appear
avoiding
close
emotions
found
genetic

happier
higher
joy
largely
less
level
miserable

recognition
relationship
researchers
run
studies
unhappiness

"You'd think that the (1)_____ a person's level of unhappiness, the lower their (2)_____ of happiness and vice versa," says Edward Diener, who has done much of the new work on positive and negative (3)_____. But when Diener and other (4)_____ measure people's average levels of happiness and unhappiness, they often find little (5)_____ between the two.

The (6)_____ that feelings of happiness and (7)_____ can coexist much like love and hate in a (8)_____ relationship may offer valuable clues on how to lead a (9)_____ life. It suggests, for example, that changing or (10)_____ things that make you (11)_____ may well make you (12)_____ miserable but probably won't make you any happier. That (13)_____ is backed up by an extraordinary series of (14)_____ which indicate that a (15)_____ predisposition for unhappiness may (16)_____ in certain families. On the other hand, researchers have (17)_____, happiness doesn't (18)_____ to be anyone's heritage. The capacity for (19)_____ is a talent you de-velop (20)_____ for yourself.

• Chapter 2: Hidden Disability

Cloze

Read the passage on this page. Fill in the blanks below with one word from the list. Use each word once.

1. _____
2. _____
3. _____
4. _____
5. _____
6. _____
7. _____
8. _____
9. _____
10. _____

11. _____
12. _____
13. _____
14. _____
15. _____
16. _____
17. _____
18. _____
19. _____
20. _____

battle	graduate	permanent
began	infant	probable
changed	likely	reading
dedication	mental	treated
diagnosed	miracle	University
doctors	occasion	walk
gone	parents	

This is a special evening for me. Tomorrow I will (1)_____ from New York (2)_____ with a doctorate in German literature—the completion of eight years of (3)_____. A momentous (4)_____ in anyone's life, it is a (5)_____ in mine because I was born retarded.

When I was sixteen months old I was (6)_____ by a team of (7)_____ as a cretin dwarf. The doctors (8)_____ me and after one month I was (9)_____ into a normal looking (10)_____. One of the doctors told my mother that I would most (11)_____ be physically normal but that (12)_____ mental retardation was highly (13)_____.

My (14)_____ brought me back home to New York and began their determined (15)_____ for my normalcy. They became my therapists, making me (16)_____ when I crawled, (17)_____ to me day and evening. At the age of four I (18)_____ to read every book I found. The (19)_____ retardation was completely (20)_____!

• Chapter 3: The Birth-Order Myth

Cloze

Read the passage on this page. Fill in the blanks below with one word from the list. Use each word once.

1. _____
2. _____
3. _____
4. _____
5. _____
6. _____
7. _____
8. _____
9. _____
10. _____

11. _____
12. _____
13. _____
14. _____
15. _____
16. _____
17. _____
18. _____
19. _____
20. _____

affects	effects	predictor
assumption	evidence	research
birth	however	scientists
concluded	influences	studies
differences	intelligence	theory
different	permanent	time
discredited	personality	

It's long been part of folk wisdom that birth order strongly (1)_____ personality, (2)_____ and achievement. (3)_____, most of the (4)_____ claiming that firstborns are radically (5)_____ from other children has been (6)_____, and it now seems that any (7)_____ of birth order on intelligence or (8)_____ will likely be washed out by all the other (9)_____ in a person's life. In fact, the belief in the (10)_____ impact of (11)_____ order, according to Toni Falbo, "comes from the psychological (12)_____ that your personality is fixed by the (13)_____ you're six. That (14)_____ simply is incorrect."

The better, later and larger (15)_____ are less likely to find birth order a useful (16)_____ of anything. When two Swiss social (17)_____, Cecile Ernst and Jules Angst, reviewed 1,500 studies a few years ago, they (18)_____ that "birth-order (19)_____ in personality . . . are nonexistent in our sample. In particular, there is no (20)_____ for a 'firstborn personality.'"

• Chapter 4: Why So Many More Americans Die in Fires

Cloze

Read the passage on this page. Fill in the blanks below with one word from the list. Use each word once.

1. _____   11. _____
2. _____   12. _____
3. _____   13. _____
4. _____   14. _____
5. _____   15. _____
6. _____   16. _____
7. _____   17. _____
8. _____   18. _____
9. _____   19. _____
10. _____   20. _____

attitude	fault	progress
country	fighting	rates
destroy	just	successes
enough	kill	technology
entirely	lessons	ways
experts	neither	worst
fatal	preventing	

    In some (1)_____, the United States has made spectacular (2)_____. Fires no longer (3)_____ 18,000 buildings as they did in the Great Chicago Fire of 1871, or (4)_____ half a town of 2,400 people, as they did the same night in Peshtigo, Wisconsin.

    But even with such (5)_____, the United States still has one of the (6)_____ fire death (7)_____ in the world. Safety (8)_____ say the problem is (9)_____ money nor (10)_____, but the indifference of a (11)_____ that (12)_____ will not take fires seriously (13)_____.

    American fire departments spend far less on (14)_____ fires than on (15)_____ them. And American fire-safety (16)_____ are aimed almost (17)_____ at children.

    Experts say the (18)_____ error is an (19)_____ that fires are not really anyone's (20)_____.

Chapter 2: Why So Many More Americans Die in Fires

Cloze

Read the passage on this page. Fill in the blanks below with one word from the list. Use each word once.

1. _____   11. _____
2. _____   12. _____
3. _____   13. _____
4. _____   14. _____
5. _____   15. _____
6. _____   16. _____
7. _____   17. _____
8. _____   18. _____
9. _____   19. _____
10. _____ 20. _____

attitude	fault	progress
country	families	rates
destroy	just	successes
enough	kill	technology
entirely	lessons	ways
experts	neither	a list
fatal	preventing	

In some (1) _____ the United States has made spectacular
(2) _____. Fires no longer (3) _____ 18,000 buildings as they
did in the Great Chicago Fire of 1871, or (4) _____ half a town of 2,400
people, as they did the same night in Peshtigo, Wisconsin.
But even with such (5) _____, the United States still has one of the
(6) _____ fire death (7) _____ in the world. Safety
(8) _____ say the problem is (9) _____ money nor
(10) _____ but the indifference of a (11) _____ particular
(12) _____, we will not take fires seriously. (13) _____
American fire departments spend far less on (14) _____ fires than
on (15) _____ them. And American fire safety
(16) _____ are aimed almost (17) _____ at children.
Experts say the (18) _____ is learning to (19) _____ that fires
are not really anyone's (20) _____.

• Chapter 5: Acupuncture: The New Old Medicine

Cloze

Read the passage on this page. Fill in the blanks below with one word from the list. Use each word once.

1. _____
2. _____
3. _____
4. _____
5. _____
6. _____
7. _____
8. _____
9. _____
10. _____

11. _____
12. _____
13. _____
14. _____
15. _____
16. _____
17. _____
18. _____
19. _____
20. _____

acupuncture
bothered
conventional
cure
doctors
education
instead

pain
president
preventive
primary
services
since
skeptical

success
suggested
symptom
treatments
typical
visits

Millions of Americans now seek out the (1)_____ of acupuncturists, usually because (2)_____ medicine failed to (3)_____ their ills. Jack Tymann, 51, is (4)_____. Tymann was (5)_____ for 15 years with severe lower back pain. His doctor (6)_____ disc surgery, but he decided to try acupuncture (7)_____. A scientist and an engineer by (8)_____, Tymann was highly (9)_____ at first. "I went in with that (10)_____ and haven't had any trouble with my back (11)_____," he says. He still goes for (12)_____ four or five times per year—not for back pain, but as a (13)_____ measure. "It's been my (14)_____ form of health care for about nine years now," he says.

Harwood Beville, 51, executive vice (15)_____ of the Rouse Co., started (16)_____ nine years ago. His shoulder had bothered him for two years, and (17)_____ to other (18)_____ met with no (19)_____. After a few treatments, his (20)_____ was gone.

• Chapter 6: Mosquito with a Mission

Cloze

Read the passage on this page. Fill in the blanks below with one word from the list. Use each word once.

1. _____   11. _____

2. _____   12. _____

3. _____   13. _____

4. _____   14. _____

5. _____   15. _____

6. _____   16. _____

7. _____   17. _____

8. _____   18. _____

9. _____   19. _____

10. _____   20. _____

approaches	kill	protect
created	land	researchers
disease	mosquitoes	seems
enough	nets	strategy
experts	perhaps	suggesting
immune	prevention	treatment
infect	promising	

One of the more interesting (1)_____ to the problem of eradicating malaria is that of Manuel Patarroyo, M.D. In 1986 he (2)_____ a synthetic vaccine, hoping that the body's own (3)_____ cells would (4)_____ the parasite.

(5)_____ because a malaria vaccine (6)_____ far in the future, many (7)_____ are (8)_____ that attention should continue to be focused on areas like (9)_____, control and (10)_____. One new (11)_____ for controlling transmission is pesticide-treated bed (12)_____, which (13)_____ sleeping people from (14)_____ and kill any bugs that happen to (15)_____ on the net.

While many approaches are (16)_____, none have proven tough (17)_____ to stop malaria. Until (18)_____ find the parasite's Achilles heel, the (19)_____ will continue to (20)_____ millions.

• Chapter 7: The Federal System of Government

Cloze

Read the passage on this page. Fill in the blanks below with one word from the list. Use each word once.

1. _____
2. _____
3. _____
4. _____
5. _____
6. _____
7. _____
8. _____
9. _____
10. _____

11. _____
12. _____
13. _____
14. _____
15. _____
16. _____
17. _____
18. _____
19. _____
20. _____

afraid
Constitution
democratic
dilemma
easy
endanger
found

freedoms
government
hand
king
men
other
pioneers

really
solution
states
strong
too
undesirable

To create a government was not an (1)_____ thing to do. Remember that in 1787 the (2)_____ at the convention in Philadelphia were (3)_____ in the setting up of a (4)_____ republican government. They (5)_____ only knew what they did not want. They did not want a (6)_____, and they did not want (7)_____ strong a central government because they were (8)_____ of losing their own (9)_____. They certainly wanted to keep the (10)_____ as they were.

Here was a (11)_____. On the one (12)_____, it seemed that a (13)_____ central government was very (14)_____ because it might (15)_____ the people's liberties. On the (16)_____ hand, a weak central (17)_____ had proven inadequate. The (18)_____ these men (19)_____ is called the "checks and balance" system, and it is the heart and soul of the (20)_____.

• Chapter 8: Too Soon Old, Too Late Wise

Cloze

Read the passage on this page. Fill in the blanks below with one word from the list. Use each word once.

1. _____

2. _____

3. _____

4. _____

5. _____

6. _____

7. _____

8. _____

9. _____

10. _____

11. _____

12. _____

13. _____

14. _____

15. _____

16. _____

17. _____

18. _____

19. _____

20. _____

after
age
allowed
care
compares
determined
even

infirmity
insists
modest
operation
pilots
profession
students

such
supposed
unprecedented
until
wait
worked

When is a teacher too old to teach? Airline (1)_____ start losing their reflexes as they (2)_____, and senility and (3)_____ can be incapacitating in any (4)_____. But philosophers are (5)_____ to just get wiser as they get older. Bertrand Russell (6)_____ into his 90s, Kant into his 70s and Socrates (7)_____ he was about 70. Weiss is (8)_____ to get his job back, (9)_____ if it means a messy lawsuit.

Indeed, Weiss can't (10)_____ to go to court. Father William Byron, Catholic's president, (11)_____ that the university went out of its way to (12)_____ for Weiss. He says that Catholic U. (13)_____ Weiss to teach students out of his apartment (14)_____ he was slowed down by a back (15)_____ two years ago. (16)_____ an arrangement is "absolutely (17)_____," Father Byron told *The Washington Post*. "False!" cries Professor Weiss. "Wittgenstein had (18)_____ come to his rooms at Cambridge," he declares. Weiss is not (19)_____ about the company he keeps. He also (20)_____ himself to Plato.

Cloze

Read the passage on this page. Fill in the blanks below with one word from the list. Use each word once.

1. ____
2. ____
3. ____
4. ____
5. ____
6. ____
7. ____
8. ____
9. ____
10. ____
11. ____
12. ____
13. ____
14. ____
15. ____
16. ____
17. ____
18. ____
19. ____
20. ____

after	infirmity	such
age	insist	suppose
allowed	model	underestimated
care	operation	quit
complains	pilot	work
determined	profession	
even	situation	

With is at age too old to become Airline (1) ____ pilots raising then retire as they (2) ____ and ability and (3) ____ can be increasing as they age. The (4) ____ airline pilots are ____ to (5) ____ to quit not after so they get older. Herman Keyzell ____ ____ into his 90s, on into his 70s and sees us (6) ____ He was about 70. We've (7) ____ to set his job back. ____ it means a loss. Lawsuit ____ ____ ____ held (8) workers can (9) ____ to provide that rather William Dixon, Catholic's president. (10) ____ that the university wanted out of its way to (11) ____ forever is says that Catholic. that ____ to (12) ____ were information of his pheasant (13) ____ he was slowed down by a bad (14) ____ ____ 59 years ago. "Oh if ____ ____ retirement is absolutely ____ ____ ____ their lives told the National ____ too for false," "people say we'll "William said had (15) ____ complains remnant Catholic. "he declare first." her (16) ____ about. A company he keep." he said (17) ____ himself to date.

• Chapter 9: The Pursuit of Excellence

Cloze

Read the passage on this page. Fill in the blanks below with one word from the list. Use each word once.

1. _____

2. _____

3. _____

4. _____

5. _____

6. _____

7. _____

8. _____

9. _____

10. _____

11. _____

12. _____

13. _____

14. _____

15. _____

16. _____

17. _____

18. _____

19. _____

20. _____

attracted
campuses
colleges
community
countries
emphasis
envy

equal
expected
flexibility
flooded
followed
foreigners
impossible

initially
practice
provide
students
troubles
undergraduate

If sheer numbers (1)_____ any proof, America's universities and (2)_____ are the (3)_____ of the world. For all their abiding (4)_____, the United States' 3,500 institutions were (5)_____ with 407,530 students from 193 different (6)_____ last year. Asia led the way with 39,600 (7)_____ from China and 36,610 from Japan, (8)_____ by India and Canada. Many of the (9)_____ entered graduate and (10)_____ programs in roughly (11)_____ numbers.

Americans take academic (12)_____ for granted, but foreigners do not. To French students, who are commonly (13)_____ at age 16 to select both a university and a specific course of study, the American (14)_____ of jumping not only from department to department but also from school to school seems a luxury. Japanese students find it all but (15)_____ to transfer credits from one school to another. Thus students who (16)_____ enter a junior college and subsequently decide to earn a bachelor's degree must head overseas.

Many are (17)_____ not only to the academic programs at a particular U.S. college but also to the larger (18)_____, which affords the chance to soak up the surrounding culture. Few foreign universities put much (19)_____ on the cozy communal life that characterizes American (20)_____: from clubs and sports teams to student publications and theatrical societies.

• Chapter 10: Antarctica: Whose Continent Is It Anyway?

Cloze

Read the passage on this page. Fill in the blanks below with one word from the list. Use each word once.

1. _____
2. _____
3. _____
4. _____
5. _____
6. _____
7. _____
8. _____
9. _____
10. _____

11. _____
12. _____
13. _____
14. _____
15. _____
16. _____
17. _____
18. _____
19. _____
20. _____

agreement
all
Antarctica
Argentina
claims
continent
countries

effect
established
explorations
however
long
number
question

remains
research
science
scientists
temporarily
useless

Until (1)_____ began the first serious study of the (2)_____ during the 1957–58 International Geophysical Year (IGY), a multi-country cooperative (3)_____ project, Antarctica was dismissed as a vast, (4)_____ continent.

Based upon early (5)_____ and questionable land grants, seven (6)_____, including Great Britain, Chile, and (7)_____, claim sovereignty over vast tracts of the continent. (8)_____, as IGY wound down, the (9)_____ of who owns (10)_____ came to a head. The 12 participating countries reached an international (11)_____, the Antarctic Treaty, which took (12)_____ in June 1961. The (13)_____ has since grown, making 39 in (14)_____. It (15)_____ Antarctica as a "continent for (16)_____ and peace," and (17)_____ sets aside all (18)_____ of sovereignty for as (19)_____ as the Treaty (20)_____ in effect.

• Chapter 11: A Messenger From the Past

Cloze

Read the passage on this page. Fill in the blanks below with one word from the list above the passage. Use each word once.

1. _____
2. _____
3. _____
4. _____
5. _____
6. _____
7. _____
8. _____
9. _____
10. _____

11. _____
12. _____
13. _____
14. _____
15. _____
16. _____
17. _____
18. _____
19. _____
20. _____

ancestral	details	probably
authority	die	remainder
circumstances	evidence	revealed
civilizations	exploration	society
clearly	furthermore	starve
contained	hunting	unlike
culture	illness	

(1)_____ the Egyptians and Mesopotamians of the time, who had more advanced (2)_____ with cities and central (3)_____, the Ice Man and his countrymen lived in a (4)_____ built around small, stable villages. He (5)_____ spoke in a tongue (6)_____ to current European languages. (7)_____, though he was a member of a farming (8)_____, he may well have been (9)_____ when he died, to add meat to his family's diet. X-rays of the quiver showed that it (10)_____ 14 arrows. While his backpack was empty, careful (11)_____ of the trench where he died (12)_____ remnants of animal skin and bones at the same spot where the pack lay. There was also the (13)_____ of a pile of berries. (14)_____ the man didn't (15)_____ to death.

So why did the Ice Man (16)_____? If injury or (17)_____ caused the Ice Man's death, an autopsy on the 4,000-year-old victim could turn up some clues. The (18)_____ of his death may have preserved such (19)_____, as well as other (20)_____ of his life.

• Chapter 12: Is Time Travel Possible?

Cloze

Read the passage on this page. Fill in the blanks below with one word from the list. Use each word once.

1. _____

2. _____

3. _____

4. _____

5. _____

6. _____

7. _____

8. _____

9. _____

10. _____

11. _____

12. _____

13. _____

14. _____

15. _____

16. _____

17. _____

18. _____

19. _____

20. _____

concept	move	still
contrary	part	survive
experiments	predicted	than
faster	return	time
future	slows	waits
light	space	yet
motion	speed	

(1)_____ to the old warning that time (2)_____ for no one, (3)_____ slows down when you are on the move. It also (4)_____ down more as you move (5)_____, which means astronauts someday may (6)_____ so long in (7)_____ that they would (8)_____ to an Earth of the distant (9)_____. If you could move at the (10)_____ of light, 186,282 miles a second, your time would stand (11)_____. If you could move faster (12)_____ light, your time would (13)_____ backward.

Although no form of matter (14)_____ discovered moves as fast or faster than (15)_____, scientific (16)_____ have confirmed that accelerated (17)_____ causes a voyager's, or traveler's, time to be stretched. Albert Einstein (18)_____ this in 1905, when he introduced the (19)_____ of relative time as (20)_____ of his Special Theory of Relativity.

Answer Key

Chapter 1:
The Paradox of Happiness

Exercise A

1. T
2. F. There is little relationship between the two.
3. F. Researchers have found that unhappiness is inherited.
4. T
5. F. It is possible to increase your happiness.
6. T

Exercise B

1. a. 1
   b. 2
2. c
3. unhappy
4. a. 3
   b. 1
   c. 1
5. a. It is the capacity to enjoy life.
   b. The sentence states that happiness is "defined as the capacity to enjoy life", and it is between dashes.
   c. to emphasize how long some of the twins have been apart
6. a
7. a. going to a movie, talking with friends, playing cards
   b. because these activities follow a dash after the words "everyday pleasures"
8. a. 2
   b. 3

Exercise C

Part 1

1. a. appears
   b. appearance
2. a. avoids
   b. avoidance
3. a. existence
   b. exists
4. a. doesn't resemble
   b. resemblance
5. a. assistance
   b. don't assist
6. a. performs
   b. performance

Part 2

1. a. indicates
   b. indication
2. a. participate
   b. participation
3. a. definition
   b. define
4. a. recognizes
   b. recognition
5. a. implies
   b. implication

Exercise D

1. (2) acknowledgment
2. (5) intimate
3. (6) spend
4. (2) a person's natural qualities of mind and character

Exercise E

I. What New Research Shows About Happiness and Unhappiness
  A. The tendency to feel unhappy may be in your genes
  B. We can create happiness for ourselves
  C. There is little relationship between happiness and unhappiness
II. Studies on the Role of Genetics in Happiness and Unhappiness
  A. University of Southern California
    1. subjects: 899 individuals (identical and fraternal twins, grandparents, parents, and young adult offspring)
    2. results: family members resembled each other more in their levels of unhappiness than in their levels of happiness
    3. conclusion: there is a genetic component to unhappiness
  B. University of Minnesota
    1. subjects: twins, some raised together, some raised apart
    2. results:
      a. in terms of happiness, twins raised apart were less alike than twins raised together
      b. in terms of unhappiness, twins raised apart were similar
    3. conclusion: there is a genetic component to unhappiness
III. The Implications of the Studies on Happiness and Unhappiness
  A. Genes only predispose a person to unhappiness
  B. We can increase our happiness through our own actions
IV. Arizona State University Experiment on Happiness
  A. subjects: students at Arizona State University
  B. experiment:
    1. students were asked to list favorite activities
    2. half the students increased these activities, and half did not
  C. result: students who did more of the things they enjoyed were happier than the students who did not

D. conclusion: the pleasure we get from life is largely ours to control

Exercise F

1. Researchers believe that there is little relationship between unhappiness and happiness, and that unhappiness is inherited but happiness is not.
2. Researchers at the University of Southern California studied 899 identical and fraternal twins, grandparents, parents, and young adult offspring with regard to happiness and unhappiness. They found that family members resembled each other more in their levels of unhappiness than in their levels of happiness.
3. Students at Arizona State University were asked to list favorite activities. Half the students did more of their favorite activities, and half did not. At the end of one month, the students who increased their favorite activities were happier than the students who didn't.
4. We can increase our happiness by doing more of the things that we enjoy and by taking control of our happiness.

Summary

According to the findings of many studies of twins and other family members, and of experiments on happiness and unhappiness, unhappiness is inherited but happiness is not. Fortunately, it is possible to overcome the genetic predisposition for unhappiness and control our own happiness.

Exercise G

Answers will vary.

Exercise H

Answers will vary.

Chapter 2: Hidden Disability

Exercise A

1. F. She will graduate tomorrow.
2. T
3. F. She learned to read when she was four years old.
4. F. Her classmates treated her very badly in school.
5. T
6. T
7. T

Exercise B

1. Lynnie Ozer's completion of a doctorate in German literature.
2. a. 2
   b. 1
3. a
4. a. probable
   b. 2
   c. 3
5. b
6. a. an illness that is not obvious, such as diabetes and epilepsy
   b. The sentence following the words "hidden disability" gives an explanation and examples.
   c. 2
7. a
8. b
9. that she was unfulfilled creatively
10. c

Exercise C

Part 1
1. a. didn't accomplish
   b. accomplishments
2. a. settlement
   b. settled
3. a. didn't develop
   b. developments
4. a. discouragement
   b. discouraged
5. a. enjoyed
   b. enjoyment

Part 2
1. a. didn't change (v.)
   b. changes (n.)
2. a. promise (n.)
   b. promised (v.)
3. a. experiences (n.)
   b. didn't experience (v.)
4. a. excuses (n.)
   b. excused (v.)
5. a. estimated (v.)
   b. estimate (n.)

Exercise D

1. (1) give up her time and energy
2. (4) gave medical care to
3. (1) changed in appearance
4. (1) get the better of; defeat

Exercise E

Infancy and early childhood:
what the doctors did
  1. diagnosed Lynnie as a cretin dwarf
  2. treated her
what Lynnie's parents did
  1. became her therapists
  2. made her walk when she crawled
  3. read to her day and evening
what Lynnie did
  1. began to read at the age of 4
  2. At 5 she could not walk without falling.
what Lynnie's peers did
  1. Other children would have nothing to do with her.
School years: 9 years old to 19 years old:
what Lynnie's parents did
  1. tried to be companions to her
  2. gave her voice and piano lessons
  3. Her mother discouraged her, but her father encouraged her.
what Lynnie did
  1. She had leading roles in musicals.
  2. She dreamed of being a great star.
what Lynnie's peers did
  1. When Lynnie was a child, her peers constantly rejected her.
  2. As a teenager, Lynnie had some status because of her voice.
College years:
what Lynnie's parents did
  1. Her father died just before she entered college.
what Lynnie did
  1. She completed undergraduate work in singing and drama with high honors.
Post college years:
what Lynnie's parents did
  1. Her mother paid her tuition toward a doctorate degree.

what Lynnie did
1. She spent 7 years abroad teaching, translating, and singing in concerts.
2. She took a graduate degree in medical translation.
3. She worked in Munich as translator.
4. She returned to N.Y. and worked as a bilingual administrative assistant.
5. She studied for a doctorate degree in German literature.

Exercise F

1. a. She was diagnosed as a cretin dwarf.
   b. They became her therapists, making her learn to walk and teaching her to read.
2. a. They treated her badly.
   b. They explained her condition to her and tried to be her companions. They gave her voice and piano lessons.
3. She overcame her disability. She worked in Europe in the medical field. She became very well educated.

Summary

Lynnie Ozer is a woman who overcame a severe but hidden disability and achieved education and success in her life.

Exercise G

Answers will vary.

Exercise H

Answers will vary.

Chapter 3: The Birth-Order Myth

Exercise A

1. F. The firstborn child in the family is not different from the other children.
2. F. Studies will probably find that birth order does not affect personality.
3. T
4. F. Growing up in a small family does not have disadvantages. Or: Growing up in a small family has advantages.

5. T
6. T

Exercise B

1. a. 1
   b. 2
2. b
3. c
4. a. 1
   b. 3
   c. 2
5. a. 1
   b. 2
6. consider; think about
7. a. for emphasis
   b. 3
   c. 2
   d. because of **for instance**
8. a. the Scholastic Aptitude Test
   b. There is a number after SAT that indicates more information is at the bottom of the page.
   c. 2
   d. 3
   e. for emphasis
9. a
10. b
11. c

Exercise C

Part 1
1. a. will encourage
   b. encouragement
2. a. achievements
   b. will not achieve
3. a. improvements
   b. will improve
4. a. stated
   b. statement
5. a. treat
   b. treatments

Part 2
1. a. competent
   b. competence
2. a. intelligence
   b. intelligent
3. a. permanent
   b. permanence
4. a. significant
   b. significance
5. a. difference
   b. different

Exercise D

1. (1) fundamental
2. (2) say it is a fact
3. (3) sets; determines; decides
4. (2) help the progress of

Exercise E

I. The Myth and the Reality About Birth Order
   A. The Myth: birth order strongly affects personality, intelligence, and achievement
   B. The Reality: this myth is not true
II. The Findings of Studies on Birth Order and Personality and Intelligence
   A. The findings of Cecile Ernst and Jules Angst
      1. Birth-order differences in personality are nonexistent
      2. There is no evidence for a firstborn personality
   B. The findings of Judith Blake
      1. Birth order does not affect intelligence; she looked at birth patterns before 1938 and compared them to SAT scores for that group of children, and she found no connection
III. Other Factors Affecting Personality and Intelligence
   A. Number of siblings
      1. It does affect intelligence; small families tend to be more supportive of the kind of verbal ability that helps people succeed in school
   B. Parents' expectations
      1. Parents who believe that firstborns are more capable or deserving may treat them differently, thus setting up a self-fulfilling prophecy
   C. Spacing between siblings
      1. Some psychologists believe there are more advantages to having kids far apart
      2. One study found that a firstborn was more likely to have high self-esteem if his or her sibling was *less* than two years younger

IV. Conflicting Research Regarding Family Size and Personality
   A. You're more likely to be outgoing, well adjusted, and independent if you grew up with few or no siblings
   B. Two studies found no differences on the basis of family size alone
   C. One study indicated that spacing had no effect on social competence

Exercise F

1. a. They believe that birth order affects personality, intelligence, and achievement.
   b. Birth order does not seem to affect personality, intelligence, or achievement.
2. Birth order differences in personality and intelligence do not seem to exist; there is no evidence for a firstborn personality.
3. a. number of siblings: it seems that having few or no siblings has a positive effect on personality and intelligence
   b. parents' expectations: they may treat children differently, setting up a self-fulfilling prophecy
   c. spacing between siblings: there are emotional advantages for children if they are spaced far apart
4. The results of research about family size and birth were very different.

Summary

Hundreds of studies have been done on the effects of birth order on personality, intelligence and achievement. Because many of the studies came up with conflicting results, it seems that the effect of birth order on these factors is a myth.

Exercise G

Answers will vary.

Exercise H

Answers will vary.

Unit I Review

Exercise I

Achievement/ Success	Health/ Medicine	Feelings/ Emotions
ability	diagnosis	discouragement
achievement	disability	enjoyment
ambition	disease	encouragement
competition	experiment	failure
dedication	genetics	gratitude
independence	heredity	misery
motivation	prognosis	self-esteem
talent	retardation	selfishness
triumph	treatment	triumph
wisdom		unfulfillment
		unhappiness
		well-being

Exercise J

Across
5. rivalry
8. paradox
9. siblings
12. no
16. to
17. range
18. status
19. emotions
23. offspring
25. that
26. fortunate
29. environment
31. one
33. assumption

Down
1. promote
2. over
3. privilege
4. peers
6. only
7. illness
10. solution
11. hardships
13. doctorate
14. hit
15. coexist
20. evidence
21. top
22. fraternal
24. stop
27. he
28. was
30. ran
32. am

Exercise K

Answers will vary.

Chapter 4: Why So Many More Americans Die in Fires

Exercise A
1. T
2. T
3. F. Children start very few of the fires that occur in the United States. Or: Adults start most of the fires that occur in the United States.
4. T
5. F. In France, insurers are not allowed to repay the full cost of fire damage.
6. F. Most homes in the United States have smoke detectors.
7. F. The high fire death rate in the United States is not the result of bad technology. Or: The high fire death rate in the United States is the result of attitude.

Exercise B
1. c
2. a. a city
   b. a state
3. b
4. a
5. a. It is very necessary.
   b. 2
6. This is not the attitude in other countries.
7. a. 3
   b. 2
   c. 1
8. b
9. a. 2
   b. 3
10. a. 1
    b. 3
    c. 3
11. a. 2
    b. 3
    c. 1

Exercise C

Part 1
1. a. important
   b. importance
2. a. negligence
   b. negligent

3. a. dependence
   b. dependent
4. a. indifference
   b. indifferent
5. a. excellent
   b. excellence

Part 2
1. a. fatal
   b. fatalities
2. a. public
   b. publicity
3. a. safe
   b. safety
4. a. responsibilities
   b. responsible
5. a. possible
   b. possibilities

Exercise D

1. (1) carelessness
2. (1) make speeches
3. (2) officials
4. (3) influence

Exercise E

People's attitude toward fires:
the United States
1. People are indifferent; they believe that fires are not really anyone's fault.
Europe
1. Public education and the law treat fires as either a personal failing or a crime.
Asia
1. Public education and the law treat fires as either a personal failing or a crime.

How countries deal with fires:
the United States
1. American fire departments are fast and well-equipped.
2. The United States spends more money fighting fires than preventing them.
Europe
1. In the Netherlands, every room must have two exits.
2. In France, insurers cannot repay the full cost of damage.
3. In Switzerland, they pay only if an identical structure is rebuilt.

Asia
In Japan,
1. penalties include life imprisonment.
2. neighbors may ask you to move away.
3. officials at fires embarrass the people responsible for the fire.

Public education:
the United States
1. Fire-safety lessons are aimed at children, who start very few fires.
Europe
1. In England, the London Fire Brigade spends $1 million a year on fire-safety commercials.
Asia
1. Korea holds neighborhood fire drills.
2. Hong Kong apartment buildings have fire marshals.
3. The Japanese learn to use fire extinguishers at work.

Technology for fire prevention:
the United States
1. There are smoke detectors in 85% of all homes.
2. Some building codes require sprinklers.
3. New heaters and irons shut themselves off.
4. New stoves will turn themselves off.

How attitudes toward fire are changing:
the United States
1. Some towns fine people if they have serious fires because they let smoke detectors go dead.
2. A landlord was charged with manslaughter because his building burned and people died.

Exercise F

1. In the United States, people believe that fires aren't anyone's fault, but in other countries, fires are treated as a personal failing or a crime.
2. The United States does not rely on people. Instead, it relies on technology, for example, sprinkler systems and equipment that shuts itself off automatically.
3. It is different because in the United States, fire safety is aimed at children, but in Asia and Europe, it is aimed at adults.
4. Some towns are fining people who have serious fires because they let smoke detectors go dead. Additionally, a landlord was charged with manslaughter when tenants were killed.

Summary

In the United States, people believe that fires aren't anyone's fault, and rely on technology for fire prevention. In Europe and Asia however, people treat fires as a crime. They educate adults in fire prevention and have strict laws.

Exercise G

Answers will vary.

Exercise H

Answers will vary.

Chapter 5: Acupuncture: The New Old Medicine

Exercise A

1. F. Dr. Gong is an acupuncturist.
2. T
3. F. Dr. Gong's office is on Mott Street.
4. F. Dr. Gong knows how to speak English.
5. T
6. F. Jack Tymann continues to visit an acupuncturist even though his back doesn't hurt anymore. Or: He continues to visit an acupuncturist to prevent his back from hurting.
7. T

Exercise B

1. slipped into
2. b
3. c
4. orthopedist
5. a
6. care; therapy; cure
7. b
8. a
9. a. 2
   b. 1
   c. 3
10. a. a life force
    b. the use of the word "called"
11. b
12. a. 3
    b. 1
13. b
14. c

Exercise C

Part 1
1. a. didn't explain
   b. explanation
2. a. recommended
   b. recommendations
3. a. stimulation
   b. stimulate
4. a. concluded
   b. conclusion
5. a. haven't decided
   b. decisions

Part 2
1. a. extreme
   b. extremely
2. a. strangely
   b. strange
3. a. involuntary
   b. involuntarily
4. a. adequate
   b. adequately
5. a. usually
   b. usual

Exercise D

1. (3) arrived at the opinion
2. (2) hurried; rushed
3. (1) is unsuccessful
4. (2) sudden

Exercise E

I. The Author's Thoughts About His First Acupuncture Experience
   A. How the treatment felt
      1. no discomfort or pain
      2. a mild warming sensation
   B. Why he had come to Dr. Gong's office
      1. the pain in his left elbow
      2. no luck with Fifth Avenue neurologist or tests
II. A Description of Today's Acupuncturists
   A. As likely to be on Park Avenue as on Mott Street
   B. As likely to be Caucasian as Oriental
   C. Most are certified; many are M.D.s or dentists
III. A Description of Acupuncture
   A. Body has more than 800 acupuncture points

B. A life force called *qi* (pronounced CHEE) circulates through the body
C. Points on the skin are connected to specific organs
D. Acupuncture points are stimulated to balance the circulation of qi
E. Acupuncture is at least 2,200 years old, but nobody really knows how it works
IV. Who Gets Acupuncture Treatments
   A. number of people: millions of Americans
   usual reason: conventional medicine didn't cure them
   B. examples of people who have acupuncture treatments:
      1. Jack Tymann, for lower back pain
      2. Harwood Beville, for his shoulder
V. Uses of Acupuncture
   A. anxiety, depression, back pain, smoking, high blood pressure, stress
   B. drug addiction
VI. Effectiveness of Acupuncture
   A. effective in four to six weeks

Exercise F

1. because he hadn't been cured, or even diagnosed, by the Fifth Avenue neurologist
2. Acupuncture is a traditional form of medicine. A life force called *qi* circulates throughout the body. There are about 800 acupuncture points on the skin, which are connected to specific organs; these points are stimulated to balance the circulation of the life force, qi.
3. a. He had lower back pain. His treatment was successful.
   b. He had "tennis shoulder." His treatment was successful.
4. Acupuncture is used to treat anxiety, depression, back pain, smoking, high blood pressure, stress, arthritis, and drug addiction.
5. Treatments usually take about four to six weeks.

Summary

Acupuncture is a traditional Asian form of medicine that has become popular in the United States. Many people, including M.D.s and dentists, have become certified acupuncturists, and many sufferers have turned to acupuncture because conventional medicine has not produced effective cures for them.

Exercise G

Answers will vary.

Exercise H

Answers will vary.

Chapter 6:
Mosquito With a Mission

Exercise A

1. T
2. F. 100 million people suffer from malaria each year. Or: Two million people die of malaria each year.
3. T
4. T
5. F. Researchers haven't found a vaccine for malaria yet.
6. F. Specially treated bed nets can prevent malaria.

Exercise B

1. b
2. a. 2
   b. 1
3. Because southern Africa refers to a general area of Africa, but Southeast Asia refers to a specific location.
4. a
5. b
6. malaria
7. a. It is an organism that grows and feeds on or in a different organism but which contributes nothing to the survival of that organism.
   b. because there is a reference to the footnote at the bottom of the page that gives the definition of **parasite**
   c. 2

8. c
9. b
10. a
11. c
12. b
13. b
14. possible plans of attack for a vaccine
15. a. It is a weed used in traditional Chinese medicine to treat fever.
   b. The comma after "qing-hao" introduces an explanation.

Exercise C

Part 1
1. a. doesn't cure (v.)
   b. cure (n.)
2. a. focused (v.)
   b. focus (n.)
3. a. gain (n.)
   b. didn't gain (v.)
4. a. is going to release (v.)
   b. releases (n.)
5. a. hasn't signaled (v.)
   b. signal (n.)

Part 2
1. a. impossible
   b. impossibility
2. a. reality
   b. real
3. a. fatal
   b. fatalities
4. a. individual
   b. individuality
5. a. able
   b. ability

Exercise D

1. (4) intensity
2. (2) is increasing
3. (1) sets free
4. (4) make way very suddenly

Exercise E

Stage #1: Parasites travel to the liver: they hide from the immune system.
Stage #2: Parasites leave the liver: they attack red blood cells.
Stage #3: Red blood cells burst: more parasites are released.
Plan #1: It would create antibodies (in humans) that would be ingested by the mosquito and stop the mature parasites from developing.

Plan #2: It would kill parasites before they enter the liver and while they are in the liver.
Plan #3: It would destroy infected blood cells.

Exercise F

1. People get malaria from the bite of an infected mosquito.
2. First, a mosquito bites a person. Then, the parasites travel to the liver, where they hide and multiply. Next, the parasites leave the liver and attack the red blood cells. After that, the red blood cells burst and more parasites are released. This is when the symptoms of malaria begin.
3. Researchers are trying to develop vaccines that would kill the parasite at different stages in its life cycle. One vaccine would create antibodies in humans that would be ingested by the mosquito and stop the mature parasites from developing. Another vaccine would kill parasites before they enter the liver and while they are in the liver. A third vaccine would destroy the infected red blood cells.
4. Each vaccine plan would affect a different stage in the parasite's life cycle.

Summary

After being almost eliminated in the world through effective spraying and drug distribution programs, malaria is making a serious comeback. It is causing illness and death to over 100 million people throughout the world. Researchers are working to develop an effective vaccine that will kill the parasite that causes malaria at different stages in its life cycle.

Exercise G

Answers will vary.

Exercise H

Answers will vary.

Unit II Review

Exercise I

Discussion/ Advice	Custom/ Culture	Illness
conclusion	attitude	ailment
decision	decade	arthritis
expert	education	cure
explanation	individual	depression
fault	medicine	disease
importance	myth	fatality
prevention	region	medicine
recommendation	tradition	pain
responsibility		surgery
strategy		symptom
suggestion		treatment

Exercise J

Across

1. conventional
4. up
6. she
10. yes
13. indifferent
14. negligence
16. ailment
18. treatment
19. but
23. on
26. it
27. ineffective
28. parasite
30. no
31. arson
32. ill
35. attitude
36. surgery

Down

2. vaccine
3. in
5. prevent
7. eradication
8. had
9. can
11. penalty
12. precaution
15. error
17. men
20. antibodies
21. off
22. diagnosis
24. certified
25. deter
28. paid

29. so
33. lose
34. are
35. all

Exercise K

Answers will vary.

Chapter 7:
The Federal System of Government

Exercise A

1. F. The United States became independent in 1776.
2. T
3. T
4. F. The U.S. Constitution described three branches of the government: the legislative, the judicial, and the executive.
5. T
6. F. A bill can still become a law if the Congress passes it again by a two-thirds majority vote.

Exercise B

1. a
2. a. independence from British domination
   b. the Continental Congress
3. a. 2
   b. 1
   c. 1
4. c
5. a. 3
   b. 1
   c. 2
   d. 3
6. b
7. It was not given control to pass tax laws, to have the sole authority to coin money for use by the states, or to regulate trade between the states.
8. a. 2
   b. because the system of government under the Articles of Confederation was not working out
9. c
10. a. 3
    b. 1
    c. the checks and balance system
11. b
12. a. A bill is what a law is called before it is signed by the president.

b. because there is a reference to the footnote at the bottom of the page that gives the definition of a **bill**
c. footnote
13. a. refuse to sign into law
   b. 3
   c. 1
14. a. He was the principal writer of the Declaration of Independence and the third president of the United States.
   b. in a footnote at the bottom of the page

Exercise C

Part 1
1. a. will establish
   b. establishment
2. a. didn't agree
   b. agreement
3. a. replacement
   b. replaced
4. a. didn't pay
   b. payments
5. a. enforcement
   b. don't enforce

Part 2
1. a. reluctant
   b. reluctance
2. a. vigilant
   b. vigilance
3. a. resistant
   b. resistance
4. a. distance
   b. distant

Exercise D

1. (4) principle
2. (2) legislative bodies
3. (2a) remove from existence
4. (3) restraint; limit

Exercise E

I. The Origin of the Federal System of Government
   A. In 1775, the war against the British began; there was no central American government established by law
   B. The Continental Congress existed but had no legal power
   C. Legal governments in the states were established to replace colonial rule
   D. In 1781 the Articles of Confederation were adopted, but the government had very restricted authority
II. The Constitution of the United States
   A. Its purpose: to insure freedom for the citizens of the United States for all time
   B. The feelings of the writers of the Constitution:
      1. They did not want a king
      2. They did not want a strong central government
      3. They wanted to keep the states as they were
      4. They wanted a government that would make laws, carry out those laws, and provide justice under the law
III. The "Checks and Balance" System of the Constitution
   A. The purpose of this system: to guard the rights and interest of the people by establishing three major branches of government
      1. The legislature, or Congress: makes laws
      2. The executive: carries out laws
      3. judiciary: watches over the rights of the people
   B. The powers not given to the government belong to the states
   C. The powers of each branch are checked and balanced by the powers of the other two branches
IV. How Laws Are Made
   A. The legislature, or Congress, drafts a law
   B. The bill is passed by the Senate and the House of Representatives
   C. The chief executive, the president, either approves the bill or vetoes it
      1. If the president approves the bill, it becomes a law
      2. If the president vetoes the bill, Congress can pass it anyway by a two-thirds majority vote
   D. If someone challenges the law, the judicial branch determines whether the law is constitutional or not

Exercise F

1. a. It had a confederation.
   b. No, it wasn't successful. The Congress had little power and no money, and couldn't borrow money.
2. They didn't want a king, they didn't want a central government that was too strong, and they didn't want the states to lose their individuality and freedom.
3. a. Its purpose is to prevent any one person or group from becoming too powerful and using that power for personal profit rather than for the people.
   b. The system works by making each part of the government dependent on the other two parts in order to function.
4. Laws are made by being drafted in Congress as bills. A bill must be passed by both houses of Congress. Then a copy is sent to the president for his approval. If he signs it, it becomes a law. If he refuses to sign it, it goes back to Congress. If the bill is passed again by a two-thirds majority vote, the bill becomes law regardless of the president's veto.

Summary

The United States became independent in the eighteenth century after a revolution against British domination. After a first democratic form of government, a confederation, was unsuccessful, people drafted a new form of government based on a system of checks and balance. This system, which was intended to protect the rights of the people, is the system still in use in the United States today.

Exercise G

Answers will vary.

Exercise H

Answers will vary.

Chapter 8:
Too Soon Old, Too Late Wise

Exercise A

1. T
2. T
3. F. He wants to continue teaching.
4. F. He wants to go to court.
5. F. He was a faculty member at Yale College.
6. T

Exercise B

1. c
2. c
3. a
4. b
5. c
6. the Equal Employment Opportunity Commission
7. a
8. b
9. a. They are well-known philosophers who worked until they were quite old.
   b. The previous sentence refers to philosophers getting wiser as they get older. It is logical that the next sentence gives examples of such people.
10. a
11. c
12. b
13. a. 2
    b. students who came to Alfred North Whitehead's rooms at Harvard
14. a. the administrators at Catholic University
    b. for emphasis
15. a. 2
    b. a poor memory

Exercise C

Part 1
1. a. equal
   b. equality
2. a. infirmity
   b. infirm
3. a. publicity
   b. public
4. a. senility
   b. senile
5. a. anxiety
   b. anxious

Part 2
1. a. defied
   b. defiance
2. a. don't disturb
   b. disturbance
3. a. insistence
   b. insist
4. a. didn't refer
   b. references
5. a. insurance
   b. will insure *or* insures

Exercise D

1. (3) extremely unpleasant
2. (3) stated emphatically
3. (4a) lawsuit; action in law (legal action)
4. (3) not thinking clearly; not expressing his thoughts clearly

Exercise E

Professor Paul Weiss: 90 years old; world-class philosopher; emeritus professor; author of many books
Event: Catholic University allowed Prof. Weiss to teach in his apartment after he'd had an operation.
Catholic University's position: This permission was unprecedented.
Prof. Weiss' position: It is not unprecedented.
Examples: (1) Wittgenstein had students come to his rooms at Cambridge; (2) Alfred North Whitehead had students come to his rooms at Harvard.
Event: Catholic University demoted Prof. Weiss to teaching graduate students part-time.
Catholic University's position: The university had shifting priorities.
Prof. Weiss' position: He wants his job back and is willing to go to court.
EEOC decision: The university discriminated against Prof. Weiss because of his age.

Exercise F

1. Prof. Weiss is 90 years old; he is a philosopher, author, and professor of philosophy.
2. a. Catholic University permitted him to teach in his apartment.

b. The university said this permission was unprecedented.
   c. He said that this permission was not unprecedented and gave two examples.
3. a. The university demoted Prof. Weiss to teaching graduate students part-time.
   b. The university said it demoted him because of "shifting priorities."
   c. Prof. Weiss wants his job back, and he is willing to go to court.
4. The EEOC said that the university must reach a settlement with Prof. Weiss within a year, or the EEOC will sue for age discrimination.

Summary

At Catholic University, Prof. Paul Weiss, a philosopher, was demoted from his full-time teaching position because he is 90 years old. The Equal Employment Opportunity Commission has intervened; Catholic University must reach a settlement with Prof. Weiss within a year or face a lawsuit. Prof. Weiss does not want to stop teaching.

Exercise G

Answers will vary.

Exercise H

Answers will vary.

Chapter 9:
The Pursuit of Excellence

Exercise A

1. F. They come from Asia, specifically China.
2. T.
3. F. They attend for educational reasons and for other reasons, too.
4. T
5. F. It is very likely that students will be in direct contact with their teachers.
6. T

Exercise B

1. b
2. c
3. a
4. privileged
5. a. 3
   b. 1
6. a. examinations
   b. because students need to pass them
7. a. 1
   b. 3
8. a. 1
   b. 2
9. b
10. c
11. a. 2
    b. 3
    c. 1
    d. 2
12. a. options, menu
    b. 2
13. a. 3
    b. 2
14. b
15. b

Exercise C

Part 1

1. a. individual
   b. individuality
2. a. creativity
   b. creative
3. a. diversity
   b. diverse
4. a. national
   b. nationalities
5. a. flexibility
   b. flexible

Part 2

1. a. independence
   b. independent
2. a. difference
   b. different
3. a. dominant
   b. dominance
4. a. excellence
   b. excellent
5. a. importance
   b. important

Exercise D

1. (2) approximately
2. (3b) compare favorably with
3. (1b) customary action
4. (1) clearly show

Exercise E

Percent of high school graduates who attend college:
the United States: 60%
Japan: 37%
Europe: Germany, 30%; France, 28%; Britain, 20%
Differences between universities:
the United States
1. People can go back to college.
2. Students can move from department to department and from school to school.
3. The community is part of a student's life.
Japan
1. It is very difficult to transfer credits from one school to another.
Europe
1. In France, students are expected at age 16 to select both a university and a specific course of study.
Differences in types of colleges:
the United States
1. There are research universities, state institutions, private liberal-arts schools, community colleges, religious institutions, and military academies.
Europe
1. There is one system.
Funding for education:
the United States
1. Students pay for their education.
Japan
1. Education is government funded.
Europe
1. Education is mostly state funded.

Exercise F

1. a. 60% of U.S. high school graduates
   b. 30% of German graduates, 28% of French, 20% of British, and 37% of Japanese
2. American colleges offer education to rich and poor families, to people of any age; students can move from department to department and

from school to school; students are involved in community life. In France, students are expected to select a university and a specific course of study at 16; Japanese students usually cannot transfer credits from one school to another; the United States has different types of schools; in Europe there is only one system

3. In the United States, students pay their own tuition; the colleges compete for students, faculty, and research grants. This competition stimulates creativity. Most foreign universities have state funding; they have less opportunity to develop distinctive personalities and define their own missions.

Summary

Although many American professors and administrators feel that there are serious problems with American universities, thousands of foreign students come to the United States to study. The American university system offers them many opportunities and advantages that they do not get in their own or other countries.

Exercise G

Answers will vary.

Exercise H

Answers will vary.

Unit III Review

Exercise I

Personality Traits	Law	Learning/ Education
arrogance	Congress	authority
creativity	democracy	competition
flexibility	government	decisions
independence	justice	excellence
individuality	liability	finance
innovator	liberty	options
power	majority	participation
pride	rule	philosophy
reputation	system	privilege
vigilance	testimony	scholar

Exercise J

Across
1. dilemma
7. discrimination
10. are
11. elite
12. liability
13. recall
15. priorities
19. options
20. in
21. potential
23. add
25. lawsuit
26. majority
28. system
30. find
31. west

Down
1. did
2. excellence
3. arm
4. veto
5. reputation
6. unprecedented
8. perception
9. hire
14. legislature
16. innovation
17. not
18. stimulate
22. now
24. guard
25. last
27. off
29. me

Exercise K

Answers will vary.

Chapter 10: Antarctica: Whose Continent Is It Anyway?

Exercise A

1. F. Most scientists agree that Antarctica should be used for research.
2. T
3. F. Most of Antarctica is ice-covered.
4. F. Antarctica is a useful continent.
5. T
6. T

7. F. Most tourists feel that Antarctica should be dedicated to scientific research and to tourism.
8. F. The Madrid Protocol prohibited countries from exploring Antarctica for natural resources.

Exercise B

1. a cruise ship
2. the authors'
3. b
4. a. 3
   b. the chance to visit the most remote and unusual place on Earth
5. c
6. Antarctica
7. d
8. a
9. b
10. International Geophysical Year
11. a. 1
    b. 2
12. c
13. a
14. a
15. areas
16. when the treaty was negotiated and went through
17. nations that haven't agreed to the treaty
18. a. 2
    b. 3
19. c

Exercise C

Part 1

1. a. employment
   b. didn't employ
2. a. established
   b. establishment
3. a. government
   b. will govern
4. a. will manage
   b. management
5. a. equips
   b. equipment

Part 2

1. a. reflection
   b. reflected or reflects
2. a. has reduced *or* is reducing
   b. reduction
3. a. are depleting *or* have been depleting
   b. depletion

4. a. don't exploit
   b. exploitation
5. a. negotiations
   b. negotiated

Exercise D

1. (3) out-of-the-way, secluded
2. (3) maintain; assert
3. (3a) barred (the continent) from serious consideration
4. (3) incorporate (it) within their domain

Exercise E

I. People with Conflicting Interests in Antarctica
   A. scientists
      reason: They treasure the advantages for research.
   B. tourists
      reason: They prize the chance to visit Earth's last frontier
   C. environmentalists
      reason: They feel that increases in research and tourism will jeopardize Antarctica
   D. oil and mineral seekers
      reason: They contend the world will be deprived of natural resources
II. The Madrid Protocol
   A. date: October, 1991
   B. original number of participating nations: 39
   C. purpose: bans oil and gas exploration for 50 years
III. A Description of Antarctica
   A. Only 2.4% of its 5.4 million-square-mile land mass is ice-free.
   B. 70% of the world's fresh water is trapped in its ice
   C. Winds blow at more than 200 mph
   D. Temperatures drop to -128°. 6℉
   E. There are no villages, towns, or plants
IV. Antarctica Is Vital to Life on Earth
   A. It reflects sunlight back into space, preventing Earth from overheating
   B. Cold water from icebergs produce currents, clouds, and complex weather patterns

C. Antarctic seas are an important link in the food chain
D. Southern Ocean is home to unique animals
V. The Antarctic Treaty's Purpose
  A. Establish Antarctica as a continent for science and peace
  B. Ensure there would not be boundaries there
  C. Temporarily set aside all claims of sovereignty

Exercise F

1. There are conflicting interests because scientists, tourists, environmentalists, and oil and mineral seekers have different, conflicting plans for Antarctica.
2. It is a treaty signed by 39 nations. The nations agree to ban oil and gas exploration in Antarctica for the next 50 years.
3. It is almost completely covered with ice, is extremely cold and windy, has no villages or even plants, and contains 70% of the world's fresh water.
4. Yes, it is necessary. Antarctica keeps Earth from overheating, produces weather patterns, is an important link in the food chain, and is home to unique animals.
5. Its purpose is to protect Antarctica from exploitation and from claims of ownership, while keeping it open for peaceful and scientific purposes.

Summary

Although no one lives on Antarctica and no nation claims ownership of it, many groups of people have conflicting interests in studying and exploiting it. Treaties have been signed by many nations to protect Antarctica—a cold, icy, remote continent.

Exercise G

Answers will vary.

Exercise H

Answers will vary.

Chapter 11:
A Messenger From the Past

Exercise A

1. T
2. F. The Ice Man was discovered in Europe by hikers.
3. T
4. T
5. F. Scientists haven't examined the Ice Man yet to get genetic information.
6. F. More bodies of mountain climbers who died 50 years ago were discovered.

Exercise B

1. c
2. the Ice Man's body
3. b
4. a. a stone knife, a wooden backpack, a bow and a quiver, a small bag containing a flint lighter and kindling, and an arrow repair kit in a leather pouch
   b. 2
5. c
6. c
7. b
8. a. 2
   b. 3
9. a
10. b
11. a. 2
    b. 3
12. a
13. the discovery of an ancient body

Exercise C

Part 1
1. a. insulation
   b. insulated
2. a. demonstrations
   b. demonstrate
3. a. will explore *or* are going to explore
   b. explorations
4. a. preservation
   b. don't preserve
5. a. destruction
   b. destroyed

Part 2

1. a. alert (n.)
   b. had alerted (v.) *or* alerted
2. a. didn't repair (v.)
   b. repair (n.)
3. a. will return (v.)
   b. returns (n.)
4. a. release (v.)
   b. releases (n.)
5. a. damage (n.)
   b. didn't damage (v.)

Exercise D

1. (1a) small parts
2. (1) routine; usual
3. (1a) firmly established *or* (1c) permanent
4. (1b) severe weather conditions

Exercise E

The Ice Man:
His Body
He was tattooed on his back and behind his knee.
His Clothing
remnants of leather garments; boots stuffed with straw
His Equipment
a bronze ax; an all-purpose knife; a wooden backpack; a bow and a quiver; flint lighter and kindling; an arrow repair kit
Purpose of Expedition
maybe hunting; maybe searching for metal ore
His Society
small, stable villages; language ancestral to current European languages; a farming culture
Possible causes of death:
Starvation
No; remnants of animal skin and bones and the remainder of a pile of berries were found near him, so he probably did not starve to death.
Injury
Maybe; an autopsy will be performed on the Ice Man's body; it may show evidence of injury.
Freezing Weather
Maybe; the trench gave the Ice Man shelter; he had a grass mat to keep him warm; however, he may have been in the trench so long that he died of the cold anyway.

Exercise F

1. a. He was wearing remnants of leather garments and boots stuffed with straw.
   b. He had tattoos on his back and behind his knee.
2. a. He had everyday gear with him: a bronze ax, an all-purpose stone knife, a wooden backpack, a bow and a quiver, a small bag containing a flint lighter and kindling, and an arrow repair kit in a leather pouch.
   b. He might have been hunting, or searching for metal ore.
3. He lived in a farming culture in a society that was built around small, stable villages and spoke a language ancestral to current European languages.
4. Where he was found, there were remnants of animal skin and bones and the remainder of a pile of berries; the trench provided him with shelter, and he had a mat to keep him warm.

Summary

In September, the well-preserved, freeze-dried body of a 4,000-year-old man was discovered. His body and the everyday gear he had with him may provide important information about his biology and his society. Furthermore, since the glacier he was found in is melting, more Ice Men may be found.

Exercise G

Answers will vary.

Exercise H

Answers will vary.

Chapter 12: Is Time Travel Possible?

Exercise A

1. F. If you could move at the speed of light, your time would stand still. *Or:* If you could move faster than the speed of light, your time would move backward.
2. F. Scientists have not discovered a

form of matter that moves as fast
as light.
3. T
4. T
5. F. The closer you are to the Earth's
core, the slower you will age.
6. T

Exercise B

1. a. 186,282 miles per second
   b. 3
2. Accelerated motion causes a
traveler's time to be stretched.
3. a. 1
   b. 2
   c. particles of matter that move
faster than light
4. b
5. a
6. c
7. b
8. a. the Twin Paradox
   b. There is a footnote at the bottom of the page that gives the
name of this hypothetical situation.
   c. 1
9. c
10. because space does not actually
curve
11. It's an example of creating an
alternative history.
12. b
13. going from Earth to the Spiral
Nebula, then back to Earth
14. a. a search
   b. because a quest involves looking
for something, as in line 118,
and results in finding something,
as in line 120

Exercise C

Part 1

1. a. experimental
   b. have experimented
2. a. causes
   b. causal
3. a. survival
   b. survived
4. a. arrival
   b. arrives

Part 2

1. a. avoids
   b. avoidance
2. a. resistance
   b. resist
3. a. doesn't accept
   b. acceptance
4. a. insists
   b. insistence
5. a. exists
   b. existence

Exercise D

1. (2b) material substance
2. (3) stretch (time) in length
3. (3a) found out (came to a decision)
by reasoning
4. (1a) ponder; reflect

Exercise E

Time speeds up:
Gravity
the farther you are from the earth's center of gravity
Time slows down:
Speed
moving faster than the speed of light
Gravity
the closer you are to the Earth's center of
gravity
Time stops:
Speed
moving at the speed of light
Experimental evidence:
Speed
In 1972, scientists who took 4 atomic
clocks on an airplane trip around the
world discovered that the moving clocks
moved slightly slower than atomic clocks
that had remained on the ground.
Gravity
An atomic clock in Washington, D.C.,
near sea level, was moved to Denver,
which is one mile high. The results demonstrated that people in Denver age more
rapidly than people in Washington.
Hypothetical example:
Speed
If you travel back and forth to the nearest
star at 1/2 the speed of light, you'll be
gone for 18 Earth years. Your hypothetical twin will have aged 18 years, but you
will have aged only 16 years.
Gravity

If you live near the beach and work deep under the sea, and avoid living in the mountains or working in a high building, you will slow your aging process by a few billionths of a second.

Exercise F

1. If you move at the speed of light, time stops; if you move faster than the speed of light, time slows down.
2. In 1972, scientists took four atomic clocks in airplanes around the world. They discovered that the moving clocks moved slower than atomic clocks on the ground.
3. An atomic clock in Washington, D.C., near sea level, was moved to Denver, one mile high. The results demonstrated that people in Denver age more rapidly than people in Washington.
4. Time reversal means that you could go back in time and do something that changes the present, even preventing your own birth, for example.

Summary

Some scientific experiments have demonstrated that Einstein's Special Theory of Relativity is correct. If we can discover matter that moves faster than the speed of light, then time travel may be possible in the future.

Exercise G

Answers will vary.

Exercise H

Answers will vary.

Exercise K

Answers will vary.

Unit IV Review

Exercise I

Environment	Science/ Technology	Making Choices	Journey/ Travel
boundary	archeology	advantage	astronaut
civilization	experiment	agreement	attraction
depletion	gravity	cause and effect	cruise
destruction	preservation	employment	equipment
ecology	researcher	management	expedition
government	scientist	negotiation	exploration
pollution	speculation	speculation	hiker
resources	theory	survival	passenger
survival			return

Exercise J

Across

4. perspective
8. evidence
11. motion
13. time
14. end
16. extreme
19. exploration
20. vast
21. artifacts
24. link
26. alternative
28. win
29. if
30. speculate

Down

1. fragile
2. ice
3. circumstances
5. quest
6. corpse
7. on
9. voyager
10. preserve
12. vital
15. site
17. relative
18. jeopardize
22. frigid
23. thaw
25. bans
27. away

Cloze Answer Key

Chapter 1

1. higher
2. level
3. emotions
4. researchers
5. relationship
6. recognition
7. unhappiness
8. close
9. happier
10. avoiding
11. miserable
12. less
13. advice
14. studies
15. genetic
16. run
17. found
18. appear
19. joy
20. largely

Chapter 2

1. graduate
2. University
3. dedication
4. occasion
5. miracle
6. diagnosed
7. doctors
8. treated
9. changed
10. infant
11. likely
12. permanent
13. probable
14. parents
15. battle
16. walk
17. reading
18. began
19. mental
20. gone

Chapter 3

1. affects
2. intelligence
3. however
4. research
5. different
6. discredited
7. effects
8. personality
9. influences
10. permanent
11. birth
12. theory
13. time
14. assumption
15. studies
16. predictor
17. scientists
18. concluded
19. differences
20. evidence

Chapter 4

1. ways
2. progress
3. destroy
4. kill
5. successes
6. worst
7. rates
8. experts
9. neither
10. technology
11. country
12. just
13. enough
14. preventing
15. fighting
16. lessons
17. entirely
18. fatal
19. attitude
20. fault

Chapter 5

1. services
2. conventional
3. cure
4. typical
5. bothered
6. suggested
7. instead
8. education
9. skeptical
10. symptom
11. since
12. treatments
13. preventive
14. primary
15. president
16. acupuncture
17. visits
18. doctors
19. success
20. pain

Chapter 6

1. approaches
2. created
3. immune
4. kill
5. perhaps
6. seems
7. experts
8. suggesting
9. prevention
10. treatment
11. strategy
12. nets
13. protect
14. mosquitoes
15. land
16. promising
17. enough
18. researchers
19. disease
20. infect

Chapter 7

1. easy
2. men
3. pioneers
4. democratic
5. really
6. king
7. too
8. afraid
9. freedoms
10. states
11. dilemma
12. hand
13. strong
14. undesirable
15. endanger
16. other
17. government
18. solution
19. found
20. Constitution

Chapter 8

1. pilots
2. age
3. infirmity
4. profession
5. supposed
6. worked
7. until
8. determined
9. even
10. wait
11. insists
12. care
13. allowed
14. after
15. operation
16. such
17. unprecedented
18. students
19. modest
20. compares

Chapter 9

1. provide
2. colleges
3. envy
4. troubles
5. flooded
6. countries
7. students
8. followed
9. foreigners
10. undergraduate
11. equal
12. flexibility
13. expected
14. practice
15. impossible
16. initially
17. attracted
18. community
19. emphasis
20. campuses

Chapter 10

1. scientists
2. continent
3. research
4. useless
5. explorations
6. countries
7. Argentina
8. however
9. question
10. Antarctica
11. agreement
12. effect
13. number
14. all
15. established
16. science
17. temporarily
18. claims
19. long
20. remains

Chapter 11

1. unlike
2. civilizations
3. authority
4. society
5. probably
6. ancestral
7. furthermore
8. culture
9. hunting
10. contained
11. exploration
12. revealed
13. remainder
14. clearly
15. starve
16. die
17. illness
18. circumstances
19. evidence
20. details

Chapter 12

1. contrary
2. waits
3. time
4. slows
5. faster
6. survive
7. space
8. return
9. future
10. speed
11. still
12. than
13. move
14. yet
15. light
16. experiments
17. motion
18. predicted
19. concept
20. part

Text Credits